LONSDALE
RING CLASSICS
Ten and Out!

Series editor: Peter McInnes

Ten and Out!
A Biography of Benny Lynch

PETER McINNES

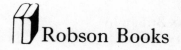
Robson Books

First published in Great Britain in 1961 by The Epsilon
Press. Reissued in the Lonsdale Ring Classics series in
1990 by Robson Books Ltd, Bolsover House,
5–6 Clipstone Street, London W1P 7EB

British Library Cataloguing in Publication Data

McInnes, Peter
　　Ten and out!: a biography of Benny Lynch.—2nd
　　ed—
　　　　(Lonsdale ring classics)
　　　　1. Boxing. Lynch, Benny, 1913–1946
　　　　I. Title　II. Series
　　　　796.330922

　　　　ISBN 0 86051 643 1

Printed in Great Britain by
St Edmundsbury Press Ltd, Bury St Edmunds, Suffolk

CONTENTS

FOREWORD

IF my father hadn't been a hard-nut Scot, dragged up almost within hailing distance of Glasgow's Gorbals though later moved south, he certainly would not have followed the Benny Lynch spotlight with the same devotion and I, as a very young boy, would not have witnessed the wee man's epic ring encounters. Reading back the book which follows and which was published at my own expense twenty-nine years ago two things particularly strike me. The first is that my memory and objectivity in recording then fistic events which had been enacted more than twenty years earlier were so much clearer than would be the case today were I trying to recount even last night's fights. The second is that *Ten and Out!* was originally written for newspaper serialisation and that, were I tackling the task today, I would go about things so very differently. But, c'est la guerre . . .

There is no question but that Jimmy Wilde and Benny Lynch are a pair who stand out way above all others as the two greatest holders of the Flyweight Championship of the World. Who was the better can only be a matter of guesswork, one of many reasons being that Jimmy's final stand came some eight years before Benny began to punch for pay. Lynch was fighting from 1931 to 1938, during which time he won the Scottish flyweight crown followed by the World, European and British titles. He captured a newly subscribed Lonsdale Belt and would probably have continued to triumph indefinitely but for the tragic physical deterioration which led to his speedy downfall and the summary termination of his ring career. Even so, he was never deprived of the World Championship in the ring.

Born deep in the slums of the Gorbals on 2 April 1913, Lynch became World Champion before he achieved his twenty-second birthday. An accomplished boxer, he hit with deadly accuracy and may well have been a greater one-punch finisher than Jimmy Wilde. He did not take chances as did the wonderful Welshman but fought with calm deliberation, picking out weak spots in an opponent's defence, then speedily demolishing his man as the foe began to weaken.

Although it was back in 1946 that Glasgow mourned the passing of its most popular sporting celebrity and more than fifty years ago when he made his final official ring appearance, little is generally known outside his native land of the inside story of this fantastic little Scotsman. His lifespan reads like fiction: a triumphant rise from the humblest of beginnings to the razzmatazz of a champion's stardom. A brief reign as king of the eight-stone men in all the world followed by a decline and fall even more rapid than the meteoric ascent. No author seeking a fistic background for a novel could concoct a more vital, human plot.

Unlike Jimmy Wilde, whose life story was ghost-written in his name years after his retirement, wee Benny never quite got around to compiling his autobiography. When he might otherwise have done so, he was too busily engaged fighting the one opponent he could never nail.

For Benny Lynch, the person rather than the super-fighter in an age of great fighters, was a tragic little figure despite the joviality and good humour he displayed when accepting the adulation of those who called themselves his friends. Tragedy was never far away from the Lynch background and he bore his lot bravely until the saddest tragedy of all—the wealth that fame brought in its wake proved too much for him. Then the numerous fraudulent friends departed and only the few true ones were at hand to try to help.

Born in poverty and the squalid side of life, the little fellow had to claw his way up, rung by rung, past scores of hungry eight-stone men in the fight game before he could begin to sample the better things which the world has to offer. These were the years of the depression and when success came it overwhelmed him. Having money to burn and being plagued by hero-worship completely ruined Benny's one-time stern ideas about athleticism and the rigours of training. He took the easy road at a trot that speedily developed into a gallop, and once he was racing towards self-destruction there was simply no stopping him.

Two years after his classic encounter with Small Montana, one year after the epic battle with Peter Kane and Benny Lynch was down, out and finished beyond all hope. Such a physical collapse seems unbelievable, but to the sorrow of every boxing enthusiast and Benny's immediate circle of true friends it was all too real.

What follows, then, is the story of a poor Scottish boy whose only real asset in life was a natural aptitude for glove fighting. His supreme artistry and power carried him to the pinnacle of success midst this astounding story of glaring fistic glory that ended in disaster through the inherent weakness of a man's flesh.

Here is Benny's authentic life story, though many of the people who made its publication possible are, inevitably, no longer with us. All those years ago I tried to produce an unbiased narrative, leaving my readers to draw their own conclusion. At best my hope is that it still makes a human tale of fighting and the fight-game, of the road from rags to riches—and the aftermath. At worst the pen-picture of a man; a man dogged through life by an ailment and finally thwarted by his early environment.

Long ago I wrote about a real fighter and my effort remains dedicated to his undiminished memory.

Part One

ALWAYS A FIGHTER

CHAPTER ONE

THE NEW WORLD CHAMPION MEETS
MR. J. BARLEYCORN

TRAINING was in full swing at the Polytechnic. The old club had suddenly assumed a new importance through having a world-title challenger workingout under its roof, and many distinguished persons were among the large crowd of spectators who had gathered for a preview of Scotland's hope, Benny Lynch.

Sammy Wilson stood talking to a London sportwriter who asked him : "These sparring-partners. I don't recognise any of them, so would you let me have their names?"

"Certainly," replied Sammy. "There's Jim Kelly, Matt Callaghan, Alex Adams, Joe Grimm, Bert Nicol, Paul Jones, Joe Beckett and sometimes I go in wi' him myself."

The reporter was unimpressed. "They're not very well-known, are they!" he exclaimed.

"Well, they're maybe no' well known to you, but they are tae me and I find that they can supply Benny wi' everything he needs. Up to now he has'na done sae badly wi' these boys, and I haven't any reason to change them. Everybody is quite happy, and that's guid enough for me."

Which was true, for a homely atmosphere pervaded the 'Poly' which was at once apparent to the visitor. Here there were no petty jealousies. Everyone fitted in and, though the schedule was hard, there was always room for plenty of good-natured back-chat.

Believe it or not, Lynch's quota of sparring at this time was around 20 rounds per day—the mere thought of which will probably make most modern-day performers tired. A notable feature of the sparring was the performance of Sammy Wilson. It's almost unheard of for a manager to act as sparring-partner but, at the risk of sending the union out on strike, I record that, in the ring before Benny's world title clash with Jackie Brown, Sammy was still as light on his feet as a ballerina and his impersonation of Jackie was the real McCoy.

Doing his roadwork around the 'Braes,' Benny was accompanied by Jim Kelly, who had first initiated him into the secrets of obtaining the maximum benefit from these exertions. Jim had done a good job, for Benny was a glutton for work and Kelly nowadays found himself hard-pressed to keep pace with his former pupil.

The entire Lynch camp had resolved that Benny should lack for nothing on the score of physical fitness and their efforts were well rewarded for, as the great day approached, their candidate was positively radiating health and confidence was the key-note.

Scotland was well represented at Belle Vue as some 2,000 Lynch supporters had made the journey to Manchester by special trains. They were a cheery crowd, but, as is usual with Scots when they travel, they made no secret of their origin and immediately before the big fight gave an impromptu rendering of the 'Auld Scotch Sangs.'

As challenger, Benny was first into the ring. He made his entry to the skirl of pipes and received a wonderful welcome. Immediately there was chaos as the well-wishers tried to get close enough to shake the hand of their idol, but the police were prepared for just such an emergency and formed a barrier as the Scot made his way to the ringside.

Police or no, one tartan-tammied Scot soon disengaged himself from the mob, darted nimbly under the outstretched arm of a burly 'bluebottle' and climbed the steps to Benny's corner. This was his old pal, Andy Smith, and in his hand he carried the same tammy which Benny had worn during a sojourn in the booths. With all the solemnity of a monarch being crowned, Benny lowered his head while Andy placed the headpiece in position.

Then, as he stepped forward to take his bow, cheering broke out anew. The tartan tammy was a symbol; Benny was fighting for Scotland.

Jackie Brown did not keep Lynch waiting, and he acknowledged the reception of his own Manchester crowd with a cheery wave of his hand and a cocky grin which spelt sublime confidence. The stage was set.

Manchester's triple champion had class, speed, boxing ability and he could punch with it. As he jaunted from his corner with the opening bell it was plain from his every movement that he fully anticipated winning.

First blow of the fight came from Lynch. As Brown, poised on his toes, came towards him, the little

17

Scot released a terrific left to the body, but the Mancunian cleverly stepped inside the hook and cracked a smart right to Benny's jaw.

Lynch hung on for a moment then, as they broke, Brown quickly stepped in again with another right intended for the same spot. But the challenger, bouncing up and down like an india-rubber ball, went back just out of reach and suddenly, with a smash that seemed to start from the region of the hip, he sprawled the champion on the canvas.

Brown rose to fight back fiercely; but Lynch ignoring—almost contemptuous of—his rival's dazzling left hand, tucked his chin well down and walked in, slinging leather from all angles. Again, the world champion went down with a thud. It seemed to be all over, but Brown, with all his precious laurels at stake, just managed to beat the count.

This time Lynch went in fiercely with wicked, punishing smashes to the liver and, game though he had already shown himself to be, neither Brown or any other man living could stand up to this. He broke ground and moved around the ring, Lynch pursuing him all the time and with the packed stadium wild with excitement and making so much noise that even hardened reporters were joining in.

For a third time Brown slumped to the canvas, this time from a left so viciously delivered to the stomach that the recipient doubled up like a clasp-knife. Yet with tremendous pluck Jackie rose to meet his foe and jolt a right to the jaw as Benny stormed in to finish it off.

But there was no steam behind that blow. The

18

Scot took it, shook his head and waded in two-handed to the body. The place was in an uproar, for it looked as though the World, European and British titles must change hands in the first three minutes of fighting. Yet at the end of the session the champion was still on his feet; but he was the only man in the hall that evening who knew what kept him upright.

He had taken a severe lacing, and as he lurched back to his stool for the inter-round refresher treatment I recall reflecting that, judging by the looks on their faces, the Mancunian's handlers needed as much reviving as did their principal. They looked stunned with astonishment.

Still, they pulled themselves together and Jackie's seconds made a good job of patching him up, so that he came up for the second still full of fight.

Carrying the attack to his man, the triple champion let loose a hail of blows to drive Lynch back across the ring to the ropes, where he then stepped in with a beautiful short right to the Glaswegian's jaw. I saw then that Brown's strength was gone for, although the blow landed right on the spot intended, its effect was negligible. Benny retaliated at once with a vicious jab to the pit of the stomach then, as Brown fell back, followed with a peculiar overhand chop to the chin. Jackie went down again.

At 'three' he dragged himself to his feet, but a left to the head deposited him once again on the deck, where he sat, looking dazedly up at referee Moss Deyong's arm tolling off the seconds above him. Fantastically game, he rose once more, but Lynch was like an avenging fury. Punches of all descriptions were flung at Brown, and he subsided under the assault. And yet, after being toppled five times, proud Brown was still there to meet another attack from Lynch. It was to be the last . . . .

Manfully, knees sagging, his battered head wagging dazedly from side to side, the Manchester boy met the Scot's tigerish rush. A right hand, starting from somewhere near the challenger's knees, exploded on Brown's pathetically exposed jaw and Referee Deyong jumped between the two men, even as Brown went down.

Then pandemonium broke loose in the stadium. Hundreds of yelling Scotsmen converged on the ring from all sides. Chaired and cheered by his supporters, the triumphant new World, British and European champion left the arena, while, shameful to have to pen, from some parts of Belle Vue came booing for the ex-champion—no doubt from the very people who had once cheered his brilliant triumphs. Why boos I do not know, for what Jackie Brown took in punishment in just four minutes thirty two seconds of fighting that night was sufficient to make him a hero even in defeat.

I stayed at the Midland Hotel after the contest and Benny, who was also a guest there, invited all and sundry to go up to his rooms and shake hands on his victory. I went and, though admittedly I was very young at the time, got something of a shock.

Entering his quarters I saw some half-dozen bottles of gin, tonics, several bottles of whisky and cases of beer. The sight surprised me, as did the presence of some characters whom I knew at once were not of the sort who should be fraternising with world boxing champions.

By coincidence Moss Deyong, who was also at the party, felt himself obliged to speak a few words of advice to the young Scot at this very moment.

"Listen, Benny, don't get a palate for that stuff," dear old Mossy said. "You're on top of the heap now, and you can stay that way a long time if you look after yourself." Then, with a disparaging wave of his hand, Deyong added: "Stay clear of alcohol if you want to be a champion for very long."

If the scenes in Manchester had been wild, they were as nothing compared to those that awaited Benny on his return to Glasgow. Twenty thousand Scots completely filled the Central Station and lined the streets outside to welcome home their hero.

Many folks thought that their champ should have been accorded a Civic Reception. Instead, one Glasgow newspaper, the 'Daily Record,' felt so strongly about it that they hastened to rectify the omission by giving a dinner in Benny's honour. To the banquet they invited the top men of the sporting world past and present—notably Elky Clark and Tommy Milligan, both of whom had come within an ace of bringing a much coveted world title to Scotland.

As he sat listening to the glowing tributes being paid to him, the kid from the Gorbals experienced a new emotion. Gradually he felt a lump rising in his throat which threatened to choke him. Doggedly he bit his lip, but this thing he could not fight so he took a wee drop instead. Then Benny bent his head low and wept.

When the dinner was at last over, the new world champion made his way to the south-side and Florence

Street. Here a strange sight met his eyes, for the dingy tenement buildings had been transformed into a blazing mass of colour. From window to window across the narrow street were stretched gaily coloured buntings, garlands of flowers, huge 'Welcome Home' placards together with the flag of every nation. Florence Street was 'en fete.' It was their day.

From here on Benny was wafted into a new world. Life became one continuous round of social functions. Between personal appearances at various cinemas and theatres, Lynch was kept busy opening bazaars, judging baby shows, beauty contests and the like. You know how it is. Everybody loves a champion, and everybody is privileged to take a drink with him. No, there was no ten o'clock curfew these days.

Meanwhile, old eagle-eye Sammy Wilson was watching quietly from the wings. He was not unduly worried for, after all, the kid was due a break, having had his nose to the grindstone for years.

But it was tough getting back into harness again, for when a boxer has been training day-in, day-out for years and suddenly lays off for a couple of months, he naturally puts on weight.

Benny returned to the ring three months after licking Brown. He was matched against the French bantamweight contender, Gaston Maton, at the local Caledonian Stadium over 12 rounds at eight-stone-six. A comfortable enough allowance for an 8-stoner, one would think, but it wasn't enough for Benny who came in one pound and two ounces overweight. As there was a forfeit clause in the contracts, that deprived him of £25 of his purse money.

The Scot ran out winner on points after a disappointing contest, for the Frenchman proved to be merely a clever spoiler who didn't carry much of a dig. Consequently he was never a menace to Lynch who was far below his best, his deliveries sometimes being badly out of distance.

Nine days later, in Leith, Benny squared up to Harry Orton of Leicester over ten rounds at 'catch-weights' (which means at no particular contracted poundage). There was much interest to see how Lynch would fare here, for Orton was of the 'southpaw' variety (one who leads off with the right hand) and about this time there was another wrong-way-rounder from the north of Ireland who had his sights set on Benny's titles. Jimmy Warnock was the name, and he had been sleeping on the champion's doorstep for some time now.

Unfortunately little information was gleaned from the clash with Orton, for though Lynch was puzzled for a while by his opponent's unorthodox stance ('corrie-fisters, they call 'em in Scotland'), he gradually assumed the ascendancy and Harry came in for a bad time of it, even though he managed to stay the full course.

Exactly a week after this, and six days before Christmas, Benny made a sentimental journey back to the Adelphi Stadium in Florence Street where Oldham's Phil Milligan had agreed to occupy the opposite corner. Phil was Northern Area champion at the time, and he had a lengthy string of knock-out victories to his credit. Once again Benny got home by the points route, though Milligan gave him plenty to think about in each of the twelve rounds.

No titles were at stake so why worry? thought Benny. In any case, he'd won, hadn't he?

This was the festive season and the time to be gay and have fun. Benny did just this. 'Fact, you could say that he and his mates really painted the town red.

CHAPTER TWO

'PERHAPS DEFEAT WILL DO LYNCH GOOD'

L IFE was good. Unlike the character in the fairy-
tale, Benny didn't have to make a choice between
health, wealth and fame. At twenty-two the lad from
the back-streets had the lot and he was the toast of
the town. At last the long years of striving were paying
dividends and, as fourfold holder of the World, European, British and Scottish titles, he felt he could relax.

As befitted a man of his standing, Lynch had
moved from the small house on the south-side and was
now installed in a comfortable villa on Burnside, a
pleasant suburb on the outskirts of Glasgow. Benny was
proud of his home and had named it, appropriately
enough, 'Belle Vue' after the famous arena where he
had become world champion.

On February 10th, 1936 his wife presented him
with a son. Nothing very remarkable about that; they
tell me it happens every day with lots of people. Yet
the way this Lynch carried on about it, you would
have thought the event was something entirely new.

Papa was delighted, and full of big plans for the
new arrival. He wouldn't be named after his father; for
one Benjamin was quite enough, thanks. And he wasn't
going to be a boxer, either. This kid was going to enjoy

all the advantages that his old man had missed. He'd become a doctor, or a lawyer, or something like that. Benny really meant it, too, but . . . .

Well, things just didn't pan out that way, but Benny was blissfully unaware of the fate which was in store for him and continued on his happy-go-lucky way. Easy come, easy go.

The weeks that followed, however, brought a couple of events that did much to upset the even tenor of the champion's life. First of these was an incident which led to the breaking of the partnership between Benny and his manager.

Sammy Wilson had been negotiating terms for a match with Irish kingpin Jimmy Warnock in Belfast. After much haggling and arguing, Sammy clinched the deal and felt reasonably pleased at having fixed Benny's end of the purse as being £300, this being the largest sum that any visiting boxer had received in Ireland up to that time, though it seems pretty meagre reward for a world champion on today's standards.

Then Lynch expressed himself as being dissatisfied with this figure and told Wilson so in no uncertain manner, ending with : "I could have done much better than that mesel!"

To which Sammy justifiably replied : "Then why did ye no' tell me and save a heap o' bother?"

Benny, more's the pity, was in one of his moods and proceeded to shout the odds, finally stamping out saying : "I'm through, washed-up and finished with the likes of ye."

Still, Sammy Wilson remained unperturbed. He'd seen Benny in these tantrums so often of late that he'd almost begun to regard them as normal. Besides, they never came to anything.

I'm afraid that this time it was different. Lynch showed up at the 'Poly' next day, not to apologise but to collect his gear and tell Sammy: "I'll no' be training here any more."

Nor did he. The champion took himself off to the Judean Club in Carlton Place, and there underwent his preparation for the Warnock fight. Meanwhile, Wilson was asking himself what happened next, for Benny and he had never had anything more than a gentleman's agreement binding their business affairs. He therefore informed the British Boxing Board of Control how matters stood, then notified Benny by registered letter that he—Sammy—would be in Belfast to carry out his managerial duties. Back came Benny's reply: "Services no longer required."

So Sammy stayed at home, while Benny travelled to Belfast to catch up with incident number two; his first defeat in some 50 fights spead over four-and-a-half years. The possibility of such a setback never so much as entered Lynch's head and he was his usual colourful self as he entered the ring that March night.

It was a big occasion in Belfast, for it was a long time since the Irishmen had seen a world champion display his wares. They fancied that their own national titleholder would be the one eventually to dethrone the Scot, and certainly Warnock's record added weight to this claim, for he had crowned a long list of successes by disposing of Tommy Pardoe inside two rounds—a task which Benny had taken seven times as long to accomplish.

Now Jimmy had twelve rounds in which to show what he could do and, though Lynch's titles were not involved since it was an overweight pairing, it was an expectant crowd of roughly 12,000 who packed the Ulster Hall to urge on their local warrior.

As usual Benny was calmly confident and apparently meant to get things over quickly, for he began the battle with a non-stop stream of hooks and uppercuts which kept the Belfast boy busy extricating himself from tight corners and hot-footing it to safety around the perimeter of the ring.

But it was not long before Warnock became more lively and gained in confidence, and when he did so he made the best possible use of his 'southpaw' stance to sorely puzzle Benny with some strong right hand punching and check the latter's headlong march forward.

Benny soon realised that he was dropping behind, but the more determinedly he attacked and the more murderous his mood became, the more erratic was his punching. And though the Irish lad was back-pedalling again, he was scoring frequently with left counters. More surprising still, when he was caught with a well-timed left hook to the chin, Jimmy did no more than blink and grin. Lynch looked blank.

Jimmy was fighting a clever campaign, and came in for a round of applause for his tricky defensive work. He made an elusive target all right and, though Benny's heavy artillery made him the boss in close quarter rallies, Warnock was wise enough to avoid such exchanges as much as he possibly could.

The real trouble from the Scotsman's point of view,

though no doubt he didn't realise it, was that his condition lacked its normal perfection and that, on account
of this, his speed and timing were just that bit off. Remember, this was the first occasion for ages that faithful
Sammy Wilson had not personally trained Benny for
a bout.

By the seventh round the latter must have thought it
was a crazy world, for the Irishman was still playing
'hard to get' and here was Benny Lynch, champion
of the entire world, chasing his man around the ring,
continually on the offensive, yet the while engaging in
a losing battle. For he was still being caught repeatedly
by Warnock's right leads and left counters, and Benny
just couldn't land a worthwhile punch on his fast-moving opponent. He was made to look very mediocre and
almost foolish.

But in the tenth Warnock suddenly seemed to be
running out of gas, and by the end of the session he
was flying distress signals. Benny tried desperately to
pull the fight out of the fire with one blow in the
eleventh, but, weary though he undoubtedly was, ringwise Warnock kept moving and, despite being badly
hurt with a couple of body blows, usually had Lynch
hitting the place where he had just been.

The twelfth and last. It was all or nothing now, for
only a KO could bring Benny victory. He was way
behind on points and he knew it. So did Warnock, and
he knew what to expect.

With the sixth sense which is a gift possessed by
all class fighters when they are in action, Jimmy must
have gathered that, though he was in dire straits himself, Lynch was also tiring rapidly. Consequently,

instead of retreating he stood his ground and traded punches with the Scot in the centre of the ring. And Benny got the shock of his life. He had never before had the awful feeling of leaden arms and feet seemingly planted deep in a bog.

It was his first moment of truth, and there and then he made a mental resolve never to step into a ring again unless he was in tip-top condition. And no doubt Benny was completely sincere in that intention . . .

A great roar such as had never before been heard in the Ulster Hall greeted the final bell and the raising of Warnock's glove in token of victory by — Benny Lynch. Yes, even in defeat the champion could rise to the occasion and, through a haze of tears, he smiled wanly and beat the referee to his decision. The Irish crowd were wild with delight.

Slowly the sad fact that he had been beaten registered itself on Lynch's brain, but after the initial shock he took his defeat philosophically. There were no alibis. He had been licked fairly and squarely but, he hastened to add, it would never happen again. You see, the old self-confidence hadn't been affected, and Benny openly attributed this setback to the fact that he had been out of the ring some eleven weeks, the best part of which period he had spent in having a good time.

'Perhaps,' wrote one leading Sports Columnist, 'a defeat at this stage of his career will do Lynch good. No one can win all the time and, without forfeiting any of his titles, he has surely been made aware of the pitfalls which lie in wait for the unwary . . . '

I believe that Benny did spot the red light, and

my surmise is borne out by his condition and performance on his next appearance, which came at Newcastle
nearly three months later. He made the journey to
oppose the local idol, Mickey McGuire, who had something of a reputation as a wrecker of champions, for he
had already conquered two of Benny's predecessors in
Young Perez and Jackie Brown.

Maybe, but it was third time unlucky for Mickey, for
May 25th found Lynch back in top gear, and the
Newcastle warrior proved little more than a human
punch-bag, the referee intervening in the fourth round
to save McGuire from the savage sorties of the Scot.

Within a week Benny visited the Capital for the
first time to demolish Pat Warburton inside three
rounds at what was then one of London's most famous
small halls, the Stadium Club in Holborn. It was something of a dual-purpose trip, the original main object
from Benny's point of view being the fact that he wished
to see Battersea's Pat Palmer in action. The Londoner,
you see, had just beaten Warnock in a final eliminator,
and was now the Board's official nominee to oppose the
Scot for the World and British titles. So, when Lynch
was offered the match with Warburton at short notice,
knowing that the opposition was not top-class he
accepted at once, probably thinking that this was a
good way of getting an expenses-paid trip to London,
seeing the sights, and at the same time of obtaining his
first glimpse of his future challenger who was scheduled
to box on the same bill.

The world champion reappeared in a Glasgow ring
in June to put the skids under Bolton's Sid Parker who,
dynamic puncher though he undoubtedly was, found the

31

Lynch fire-power far too much and was knocked out cold in the ninth round.

But the finger of suspicion was already abroad in the locality.

"Sure Benny's the hardest hitter in the business," the dismal Jimmies moaned. "That does 'na' alter the fact that since he beat Brown he's never come in at anywhere near the flyweight limit. He'll have to cut an arm off to make eight stone."

This, of course, was really idle gossip, but Benny had not helped matters by refusing to defend his European title when called on to do so, with the result that he had forfeited that championship and given fuel for rumours that he was hard-pushed to reduce to the required limit.

Happy-go-lucky Lynch wasn't in the least perturbed. After all, as world champion he was king of them all, and as British titleholder he would soon be competing for a newly-subscribed Lonsdale Belt.

Let 'em all think what they liked. He'd show the doubters who could do what when he stepped in with Palmer.

CHAPTER THREE

AND IT DID—FOR A WHILE AT LEAST

P AT PALMER had what it takes to climb the ladder in the toughest, most uncompromising and most highly individualistic career left in a standardised world. As an amateur he had won the British, European and Empire Games titles and, though he had been a professional only eighteen months he had quickly made headway, setting the seal on his talent by becoming Southern Area Champion.

A clever boxer with a heavy punch, Palmer was a typical Cockney. Cheerful, chirpy and sublimely optimistic, he made no secret of the fact that his hopes of success would depend largely on his ability to outbox Lynch. This was Pat's big chance, and he meant to make the most of it.

For the champion the occasion was no less important, for he would be placing his titles on the line. And without them Benny knew he'd be just another fighter, which would be a case of returning whence he came. Consequently, something extra special in the way of training chores was indicated.

I have already described how, since the break with Sammy Wilson, Benny had been looking after his own business affairs and working out at the Judean Club where, incidentally, he had placed himself under the supervision of Willie Lawrie. Recently, however, our fighter had acquired an establishment of his own. The new gymnasium, which he had purchased from his leather-slinging pal Johnny McGrory, was a converted shop situated in Rutherglen Road deep in the very heart of the Gorbals.

Here the kids from the south-side could worship at the shrine of Benny, for it was also the headquarters of the Olympic Amateur Athletic Club—the unpaid side of the outfit being looked after by Lynch's uncle, Jimmy Donnelly.

Uncle Jimmy merits a few words in passing. A self-effacing sort of fellow, Mr. Donnelly was never about when the pictures were being taken, but when the skies looked dark Benny could always look around, find Uncle Jimmy and, sure enough, things would straightaway begin to look up. However, more about that later on.

'Puggy' Morgan, too, made his entry at about this period. In Scottish boxing circles Morgan's reputation as a trainer was of the highest order, for 'Puggy' had been conditioning champions since way back and had nursed such men as Elky Clark and Tommy Milligan into world class. Benny badly needed a trainer at his new quarters, and he rightly considered himself fortunate in obtaining the services of this old maestro.

Typically Scottish, 'Puggy', with a dour countenance, gave no hint of the humorous nature that lay behind that dead-pan, for his wisecracks and clowning had the real professional touch about them. But on the job he was a man of action, and before long became an integral part of the Lynch entourage. Under his capable direction training camp was struck at Drymen, a small country town some 12 miles outside Glasgow.

Here, in the heart of the country, Benny had ample scope for the roadwork which he had been neglecting of late. A wooden hut served as sleeping quarters and a ring was erected in the open-air; possible because it was now mid-August and towards the end of a hot, dry summer. Plenty of sparring partners were available, and work began in earnest for the testing defence against Palmer which was scheduled for September 16th under George Dingley's promotorial banner at the vast Shawfield Park, Glasgow.

You will gather from the latter fact that, though there had been keen opposition bidding to obtain the match for London, so great was Benny's popularity and drawing-power that Dingley had been able to top the offers of all his rivals.

Among the hired-help engaged to trade punches with Lynch in his training sessions was a young English lad who was beginning to hit the headlines down south by virtue of having won each of his 25 contests to date, no less that 21 of his opponents having failed to last the distance. A quiet lad who wielded a blacksmith's anvil when he wasn't tossing leather, he didn't have very much to say, but if you asked him he would look up with his big, staring eyes and tell you that his name was Peter Kane.

Peter was combining business with business, for he was featured on the Lynch-Palmer bill versus a fellow by the name of Willie McCamley. McCamley was also a sparmate of Lynch but, being ever a diplomat, 'Puggy' saw to it that the paths of Peter and Willie did not cross. Training was completed without incident, and 'Puggy' pronounced Benny as being: "Fit to fight a whole regiment of sodjers."

Equally enthusiastic reports were emanating from the Battersea boxer's camp and a rare set-to was anticipated in this, the first fight involving a world championship ever to be staged within the borders of Scotland.

Shawfield Park, by the by, is the ground of the Clyde soccer club, and some 40,000 excited fans were crammed in like sardines when the turnstiles were shut and the 'house-full' notices displayed.

Outside the gates another couple of thousand hung about, discussing Benny's chances in the intervals between receiving over-the-wall results of the preliminaries from friends inside. Many of these were unemployed lads who could not afford the price of admission. Nevertheless, they were determined to be on hand where, if they could not witness the battle, at least they would be able to get a sniff of the big-fight atmosphere.

A polite Scottish welcome was accorded Palmer as he made his way down the aisle and, though a goodly number of his supporters had made the long trek from London, their enthusiastic chorus was as nothing compared to the swelling roar which greeted the appear of the champion. Benny was the big-shot, and why not? Tonight he was determined to give every Scotsman something to be proud of.

The Londoner was in trouble as early as the first round when Lynch, stung into action by a sharp right cross, whipped home a left hook combination to body

36

and jaw and then followed with his own right cross to the latter quarter. Palmer's eyes glazed and his legs buckled but, like the fine ringster he was, he grabbed Benny's arms and hung on until the referee ordered 'break,' by which time his superb condition had enabled him to recover sufficiently to last out the session without further upset.

It became clear in the second that the world champion was in his very best form. Picking his punches as only a master can, Lynch had Palmer wilting under some terrific lefts and rights to the midsection. But though Pat was having to stand up to to a deal of punishment, he was by no means out of the picture and, in brief spasms, showed up well as an opportunist with sudden rallies.

As the men went to their corners the huge crowd cheered loud and long and stamped their feet in applause. It was a spectacular fight, and the customers were enjoying every second of it.

Contrary to expectations, it was Palmer who set the tempo of the third session. Benny coasted this one out and was content to let the Londoner do most of the work, but when the champion did let fly with his heavy artillery it could be seen that he had the situation well in hand. I think he knew now that he was going to win, and was biding his time for the right moment to apply the coup-de-grace.

Lynch continued on the defensive in the fourth, and his grace of movement was a delight to watch as he glided effortlessly about the ring. Several times the challenger tried with his whiplash right cross, but Benny was well set now and always cleverly avoided or smothered it. Reading the signs of the Scot's inaction wrongly, Pat crowded in and rushed Lynch to the ropes, only to be made to switch from the offensive to the defensive instantaneously as, by dint of brilliant footwork and the merest deflection with his rival's right glove, Pat found himself backed against the hemp and on the receiving end of a hurtful counter.

Palmer showed some signs of weariness as he answered the bell for the fifth. The body-battering he had been subjected to was beginning to take its toll. But Pat was still dangerous, as Benny found out when he was on the wrong end of a right uppercut that jolted his head back. Seizing what looked to be his best opening yet, Palmer went to work inside and was not doing at all badly until the Glaswegian connected with a crashing left to the heart that brought a grunt of pain from the Battersea boy.

The sixth session saw Palmer tiring rapidly, and Lynch turning on the heat. Now the time had come to put over the pay-off punch but, when he tried it, his adversary came in for a round of applause as, through clever ringcraft, he made the champion miss badly with his right. And then Pat twice repeated the process with well-timed ducking. But right on the bell a left hook got home on the Londoner's jaw and caused his eyes to go blank and staring like the windows of an empty house. The bell came as his saviour, for I am certain that one more blow would have finished the fight there and then.

No man could have stood up long under the going-over which the once sprightly Palmer had to withstand in the seventh. Gradually Pat began to sag at the knees under Lynch's merciless assault. Left eye cut, closed and looking like a spilt lump of strawberry jam, the courageous contender was on the way out.

Pausing for a moment in his work of destruction, Benny gauged the distance then struck to the jaw with that devastating left hook delivered with the speed of a striking cobra. Palmer seemed to disintegrate on his way to the canvas.

"One, Two, Three, Four," yell the referee and timekeeper in unison. Then—Clang! Pat, completely unconscious, had been saved by the bell.

Feverish work by his seconds during the minute's respite enabled him to come up for the eighth, but the continuation of hostilities was designed to be short-lived. Palmer tried a couple of weak left leads, where-upon Lynch retaliated with a mighty left hook to the solar plexus and the southerner's arms instinctively came down to protect his abdomen. He was a sitting bird.

Once again Benny carefully measured his man, then up came that dreaded left hook to the jaw and Pat measured his length on the canvas, this time to writhe about as the fatal 'ten' was counted over him. A gallant challenge had failed.

The scenes that followed must surely have remained a vivid picture in Benny's mind until his dying day, for, in a glorious paean of praise, two-score thousand voices were raised in harmony as the wildly excited Scots acclaimed their champion.

Reverently, Benny was hoisted on to willing shoulders and transported through the cheering mob to his dressing-room. Vainly did the police try to check the surging mass of humanity. Finally, in the interests of public safety, an appeal for order was put out over the loudspeaker system.

"He belongs tae Glasgae; dear auld Glasgae toon," they sang out, putting the famous old song into the third person. And all were agreed that Benny Lynch was the greatest guy in all the world.

In his packed dressing-room, the object of all this adulation was strangely troubled again by the presence of a lump in his throat.

"They're a real bonnie crowd," he muttered in a husky voice. "I hope I'll never let them down."

CHAPTER FOUR

EVERYBODY'S CHAMPION AT LAST

NO riotous celebration parties followed Benny's momentous victory. He was back on the straight and narrow, and that was where he meant to stay.

It was two months to the day when he next entered the ring for a serious bout, and then the opponent was old friend Phil Milligan, who had caused Benny plenty of trouble on their first meeting about a year earlier. This time the venue was Manchester, which meant that Phil was campaigning practically on his 'own midden.'

But he soon found that he was up against an altogether different Benny Lynch, and any aspirations Phil might have had towards being recognised as a serious contender for the title were blown to pieces, the Scot blasting him completely and causing the referee to retrieve the wreckage in the seventh round.

An appropriate end to Benny's fistic year came when he was presented with several trophies during a charity show at the Stadium Club, Holborn, on December 10th. The world champion had been booked to top the bill against a useful performer called Eric Jones who hailed from Coalville in the Midlands. Immediately before going into action, Benny was given a real thrill when he accepted the Lonsdale Belt (which he had won by licking Palmer) from the hands of its founder, the late Lord Lonsdale himself.

His Lordship then presented the Scot with an inscribed silver plaque fashioned in the shape of the earth in recognition of his being world champion, and a big inscribed cup emblematic of his having won—and never lost in the ring—the European title.

As if in honour of these awards, Lynch was at his very best that night and served up a classic display besides punching with the power of a welterweight to put paid to Jones in the second round.

Everything was hunky-dory, only fly in the ointment being the fact that America had decided to set up a world flyweight champion of her own. The fighting name of this pirate champion was Small Montana, but he had been born Benjamin Gan. A little yellow-skinned manikin with a melon-slice grin who hailed from the Philippines, Montana's claims to universal recognition as world's number one flyweight were based on the fact that he had outpointed one Midget Wolgast in a ten-rounder which was recognised in some parts of the United States as having involved the title.

These claims were decidedly weak, for all parts of the U.S. had recognised Jackie Brown as world kingpin, and Lynch had conquered the aforementioned Brown before the setting up of Montana.

Still, something had to be done about it and, through the efforts of the late Sir Arthur Elvin of Wembley Stadium, Lynch and Montana were brought together to settle once and for all the question of world supremacy at his Empire Pool on January 19th, 1937.

Montana duly arrived in London, and his olive-skinned figure excited much comment. Twenty-four years of age, he stood only five foot two—two inches shorter than Lynch. Of slim build, he looked frail, but beneath his satiny skin the muscles rippled in a manner that caused the experts to put him down as being a pocket Hercules. A likeable little fellow, Montana left the talking to his manager, Johnny Rogers, and certainly he couldn't have had a more vocal mouthpiece!

"My boy's the fastest thing alive," proclaimed Johnny modestly. "Hits like a heavyweight, too. Yes sir, that title is going right back home where it belongs!"

Despite this sort of build-up Lynch was installed as a firm favourite, and the odds increased on the day of the fight, for at the weigh-in Montana came in at seven stone nine and three quarter pounds as against Lynch's seven thirteen and a half.

General opinion insisted that no man living could concede nearly four pounds to a flyweight like Lynch—for four pounds among little men is the equivalent of about a stone to middleweights and above. And, for once, general opinion was right.

The vast Empire Pool was filled to overflowing to witness a vintage contest. A great deal hinged on the result, for everyone knew that if the title went to America it would probably be a long time before it came back to these shores. The onus, then, was on Benny, for he was fighting to uphold the prestige of British Boxing.

It was a colossal responsibility, but the powerful little Scot showed no trace of nerves as he made his way to the ringside to a deafening reception. Montana had already made his entry, and he spent the duration of the lengthy preliminaries limbering up full tilt in his corner.

Not only did dour wee Benny, still only twenty-three, score a meritorious victory that night but he thrilled even the most hard-boiled of fight-fans by the classic manner in which he boxed. Any ignoramus still sceptical concerning the Britisher's class would have been forced to acknowledge him as the greatest eight stone man since the days of Jimmy Wilde.

Benny proved himself to be a real dyed-in-the-wool champion. He showed once and for all that a top-class box-fighter has no need to rely only upon putting his man out for keeps with one punch; he set out like a fine general to beat his rival in every department of the game.

Those who were somewhat inclined to fear that Montana might prove just that bit too fast for our champion soon had their fears allayed. It was Benny who set the pace, who maintained it, and who caused looks of amazement and later even of consternation to spread over the countenances of the Philippino's manager and trainer who were acting as his seconds.

The whole trend of the battle turned upon the question of tactics. Lynch adopted the correct ones for his purposes, while Montana took a line very different from that which was expected of him.

Making the running, the Scot displayed truly amazing speed of both hands and feet, and completely took the wind out of his rival's sails. Montana attempted to stand up straight and box his opponent off, but in his every attempt the tiny yellow-skinned man from Manila failed.

Certainly it must be admitted that Montana was the faster of the pair in the early rounds, but Lynch was always moving with him, stepping in and out with sound purpose, always conducting his campaign with superb generalship and showing himself to be a highly-skilled craftsman.

It was a battle for the connoisseur. One of the fastest, cleanest and most skilful I have ever seen, it was one of those contests which will for ever live in the memory of those who regard a boxing bout as the supreme test of a man's fitness, both mental and physical.

Without detracting one iota of recognition for Montana's brilliant performance, it must be made clear that he was well and truly. bested by an opponent who was not only more mobile physically but could also think more quickly.

Benny's every move was a delight to the student of the Noble Art. When he punched, he hit with the knuckle-part of the glove; when he sidestepped, blocked or parried a blow, he did so with the smooth action of a well-oiled and highly-tuned machine.

At no time was Lynch taken out of his stride. Right from the outset he must have sensed that Montana was incapable of punching with anything like the force necessary to put him away, so he set out to make the Philippino fight the way he (Lynch) wanted him to. Benny would draw his man in on to a left hook, then shift with incredible accuracy and speed to whip in a venomous right to the side of the head.

45

On no account let it be thought that the foreigner lacked class himself. Those who had had the pleasure of watching him in training were prepared to see Montana put up a clever and dazzlingly fast display. And he did so; but he was beaten by an even better man.

Yet Montana's plan of shooting out his left, breaking ground under the strong attacks of his rival and then stepping in with swift counters was capital work while it lasted.

The set-to was not only both thrilling and entertaining to the fight-fan, it also made an interesting study for the student of psychology. For the facial expressions of these two superb glove-artists afforded sufficient material for a story in themselves.

Lynch calm, phlegmatic and yet keenly alert, marking intently the effect of each blow he landed and of every move he made. Montana, renowned for his flashing smile and imperturbability, forced to express not only puzzlement and bewilderment at the swift and skilful moves of his adversary, but even distress as he found himself—and he frequently did—tied up in knots and made the target for a heavy body bombardment.

At no time did either man look in serious danger of being knocked out, yet Lynch was afforded two opportunities near the end of the fight, when he could not have been completely certain that he would win, to triumph decisively. But Benny was too gentlemanly to take them.

Both came in the fifteenth and last round. On the first occasion Montana got his head entangled in the ropes and was momentarily pinned helpless—literally like a fly emeshed in a spider's web—but instead of moving in and nailing him, Lynch stepped forward, grabbed hold of his opponent, pulled him clear and then shook hands before resuming hostilities.

Again, a few seconds later, Montana half slipped and was temporarily defenceless, but again Benny helped him to right himself, and once more they shook hands before continuing to do their best to do their worst to each other.

I have still got the notes which I jotted down that night and, while I was not close enough to the ring to judge accurately — having spent weeks saving five bob in order to get in at all — I see that I made them level after four rounds; that Lynch won the next four; that nine, ten, eleven, and twelve were shared; that Montana took the thirteenth and fourteenth and Lynch the fifteenth. I thought there was never more than a quarter of a point to choose between them in any round, so simple arithmetic will tell you that, as Benny took seven rounds against Montana's four with four even, on my count the Scot triumphed by three quarters of a mark. That may not seem much phrased in such terms, but in professional boxing bouts it constitutes the clear superiority of one contestant over another.

When it was all over, and both before and after the Scot had been named as winner, Lynch and Montana locked themselves in an embrace which spoke volumes for the sportsmanship of them both. And which was a dig in the ribs for those who maintain that boxing is a brutal sport which breeds only the aggressive instincts. It was a perfect end to a perfect fight.

Too bad there was only one world, and so could only be one undisputed world flyweight champion. For if ever there was a case of 'pity there had to be a loser' this was it.

I imagine that when America fell into line by recognising Benny Lynch as titleholder, the Scot could have laid strong claims to the title of 'Most Popular Person in Britain.' Such white-hot adulation could be dangerous, especially to a lone wolf such as Benny had been since breaking away from Sammy Wilson and conducting his own business affairs.

One person who understood this was George Dingley, an old friend who was also a leading promoter. George had been keeping a fatherly eye on the little 'un, in fact he had been helping Lynch all along the line in an unofficial capacity.

Now, suddenly, Benny realised that he needed a managerial pilot who would relieve him of all business responsibilities other than that of actually doing the fighting. What more natural then, than that willing George should be the man to fill the breach.

But if anyone had suggested after the Montana affray that Benny only had a dozen fights left in his career, and that he was going to lose four of those, the suggester would have been laughed at as insane.

Yet such was the case, as we shall see.

CHAPTER FIVE

REACHING THE TURN

THERE'S no business like the fight business. Every really good fighter has some safety-valve; some special way of getting over the monotonous grind of training so necessary for those who want to earn big pay-days; some special way of recuperating after the nervous tension that is always present prior to a big-fight.

Funny thing about pre-fight nerves. They affect different people in different ways. As the day of the big battle draws near, some men become so edgy and snappy that it's almost impossible to live with them. Others get butterflies in the stomach and can't sleep at nights. A third class have a completely negative reaction to the pre-fight atmosphere, but their unwinding comes afterwards like the spring of a clockwork toy.

Benny was one of these. Apparently he didn't have any nerves but, nevertheless, his emotions were all bottled up inside him with the result that, after each important contest, he just had to do something which would take him out of himself or bust. That is not difficult to understand.

What is not so easily understood is why a fellow who was tough and courageous enough to become champion of the world should have been so pliable in the hands of the smooth-tongued 'friends' who swarmed around him like flies in his hour of triumph. They took him racing and they took him drinking and, sad to say, Benny was not slow in acquiring a palate for both.

Save? For what? Those concrete fists of his would bring Benny in an ever-increasing flow of pound notes. His whole life was still ahead of him, he thought. Adulation, flattery, lionising and exploitation; Lynch was given the full treatment.

Let's ride along with Benny for a wee while and discover where he slipped up. Put yourself in his shoes. Would you have been able to tell true friends from phonies when you were twenty-three? If everyone insisted on telling you what a fine fellow you were would you have resented it?

No, I expect that the majority of us would fall hook, line and sinker just like this tragic little fighter did. Most of us would lap up the praise and lap up the booze, and think what nice folk they were.

Depends what you call nice people, of course. These were well-spoken, had nice clothes, used the best hotels and made out they had plenty of cash. They were 'big', and Benny was 'big'.

That type is all right when you are winning, but brother, just you take one larruping and they'll be pumping the hand of the guy who dished it out just as sure as you're born. Then you're out in the cold, plus a lot of expensive tastes and habits that are not so easy to abandon. No, it's a friend in need who is a friend indeed.

I'm jumping ahead, though, for it wasn't like that

with Benny . . . . yet. He was the best in the business, no doubt about that. But he was getting a little careless, wavering slightly from the straight and narrow trail along which he meant to steer.

A clue to this might have been spotted by a shrewd observer when he met Fortunata Ortega of Spain at the Kelvin Hall. Mind you, the Spaniard was no slouch but, though Benny won on points after 12 hard-fought rounds, the form displayed by the world champion that night was far below what might have been expected.

The Scot's timing was out, his deliveries were not cleanly landed, and at times he was made to look distinctly sluggish by the versatile Ortega. Yet this was no more than three weeks after his wonderful display in ousting Small Montana.

I'd say that the Ortega fight marked a definite turning point in Lynch's life, because, from here on in, old man trouble was always liable to raise his ugly head and was never far away.

For example, on the first day of March Benny went to Manchester and got himself disqualified in the fifth round of a non-title affair with 'Nipper' Len Hampston of Batley. Actually, it may be a trifle unfair to say that the Scot 'got himself disqualified,' because what actually happened was that his second jumped into the ring to save him from what looked like a certain knockout defeat after he had been floored some half-a-dozen times.

It was impossible to avoid noticing that Benny looked only half trained on this occasion—and even that was giving him the benefit of the doubt.

Hampston, a bantamweight, claimed a foul in the very first round when he went down from a left and right to the pit of the stomach, but when the referee began the count Len rose. Another left to the body, one of those border-line blows, immediately dropped him again for 'three' and this blow was responsible for a lot of feeling creeping in, both on the part of the boxers and of the crowd.

Another Lynch left which landed in the region of the waistline had Hampston appealing to the referee in the second, but the official ruled the punch perfectly legitimate. It was not a pretty fight to watch, for both boys were now tossing blows indiscriminately, and the Batley man sent in a shot which looked doubtfully low in the extreme.

The third was sensational. Hampston connected with a terrific left to the body, and Lynch dropped to the floor like a sack of cement. At 'eight' he was on his feet, but not for long, for the 'Nipper' crashed home another blow to the pit of the stomach and Benny sank down for another count of 'eight.'

He rose to stop another pile-driver in the stomach, and this time he took 'nine.' Benny just about beat the count, but was vainly trying to stem the hail of blows being flung at him when the bell came to his rescue.

O-o-o-h!, screamed the crowd as the world champion crumpled to the canvas yet again in the fourth following another left and right to the body. Dragging himself on to his hands and knees, Benny only just succeeded in hauling himself upright in time and then in lasting out the round.

A much weakened Lynch could do nothing more

than back away from his ever-advancing foe in the fifth. Feinting for the face, Hampson suddenly stooped low and jolted a stiff-arm right to the body to score another knockdown.

Benny was badly hurt again, though apparently his head was quite clear for, as the count reached 'seven,' he hurled his gumshield towards his corner and then rose at 'nine.'

Hampston stalked his man relentlessly, and soon let go a wicked right to the body to drop the champion as though poleaxed. Writhing in agony, the Scot struggled to his knees. One last sensation as Nick Cavalli, Lynch's chief second, leapt into the ring, frantically gesticulating to the referee and claiming a foul.

At once Gus Platts, acting as referee on this occasion, ordered Cavalli out of the ring, only for Nick to pick Benny up like a child and carry him to his corner. Pandemonium reigned. The crowd were in an ugly mood as, amid jeers, cheers, boos and cat-calls the announcer called for silence in order that he might make known the official verdict: "The referee disqualifies Lynch for misconduct on the part of his second; Hampston the winner!"

Nice goings on, I must say. But Benny Lynch, champion of the world, had no alibis. All he wanted was a return, and that as soon as possible.

And such were his phenomenal powers of recovery that, exactly three weeks later, Lynch went to Leeds and handed Hampston a terrific thrashing in ten rounds. But this was the real Lynch, a Lynch who had got the poison out of his system by burning up the roads around

Burnside and by punishing heavy bag and sparring-partners alike. Benny had had a gruelling time doing it, but the point was that he had done it.

This second meeting with Hampston had one of the most dramatic finishes I can recall. At the start of the tenth round I had the Glaswegian slightly ahead on points in my mind's eye. Benny sprang from his stool like an alley-cat. He had a scar on his right cheek which some said was the legacy of a Glasgow gang-fight, and I recall that this stood out lividly as he bowled his right arm flush to Hampston's jaw.

One of the handsomest boxers I have ever seen, Hampston went white as the blow numbed his brain. Lynch leapt forward, but before he could strike again Hampston pitched into the ropes and slithered on to the canvas. Len climbed to his feet at 'eight,' took a further barrage of punches to the head and, as Benny stood off, preparatory to leaping in again, the Yorkshire boy, who had apparently heard his seconds yell to him to take a further count, slowly bent down and put his right glove on the canvas.

Thus he was technically down, but in my opinion he should have been reprimanded for going down without a blow. Referee Jack Smith seemed temporarily nonplussed, but eventually took up the timekeeper's count and, when Hampston rose at 'eight,' he was allowed to continue. One outraged spectator felt so strongly about this apparent miscarriage of justice that he flung his programme into the ring and for a moment we thought the towel had been skied.

But the most dramatic incident of all—the knock-out—was still to come. Benny pursued his man with short accurate hooks to the body, finally switching to the jaw and catching his man with a left as he sprawled off the ropes. Hampston was knocked unconscious over the middle strand, so that the back of his head struck the 'apron' of the ring outside the ropes, and his body then see-sawed, with first his heels dragging on the canvas and then his head striking the apron once more.

It was one of the most spectacular knockouts I have seen, and it ended an evening which had a collection of positively surrealist incidents in it. First of all, in another section of Leeds Town Hall the Assize Courts were going on, and they continued so late that men were still being sentenced after the boxing crowd had invaded the main hall.

Then the entry of the two boxers into the ring was something which belonged properly to a Walt Disney Fantasia. Benny was piped into the roped square by a piper in full Highland rig. Hampston made his entry to the strains of 'On Ilkla Moor Baht 'Aht,' played on the cornet by a man in full evening dress!

Finally, it was one of those blood-stirring nights when "Lynch Law" reigned, and Benny looked invincible when he was meting out his own version of it.

Delighted at getting his revenge so completely, Benny was now bent on cancelling out the only other blot on his record—that defeat at the hands of Jimmy Warnock in Belfast.

George Dingley came to terms with the connections of the Irish boy and planned the return for an open-air show at Glasgow in June. This suited Benny down to the ground and, what was more, he was fully prepared to put his World and British titles at stake if the

Board of Control were willing to give the pairing their official blessing.

They weren't, and instead announced that Phil Milligan and Peter Kane, both of whom I have referred to previously, must meet in an eliminating contest, the winner to meet Warnock for the right to challenge Lynch.

Dingley lodged an official protest on behalf of Lynch, as did Warnock's manager acting for his charge. This was based on the fact that, should the Board's original decision be altered, both Benny and Jimmy would agree to waive the six months' grace usually afforded to a champion and meet the Milligan-Kane winner when called on to do so.

But, rightly, or wrongly, permission was still not forthcoming, probably because Warnock had recently put up several luke warm performances against men whom Lynch had defeated comfortably.

Meanwhile Jimmy underwent a course of special training at Bangor, in County Down. He declared himself to be fitter than ever before, and was certain that he would repeat his previous victory over the champion. Still awaiting the Board's final word, Warnock's only concern was whether the cherished titles would be at stake.

In the opposition camp Lynch was likewise taking things seriously. So much so that he had hired famous trainer Alec Lambert to come all the way from London to look after him, and the form he displayed in his public workouts was the subject of much favourable comment in the press.

Nothing was left to chance for, in addition to the

regular members of the camp, two 'southpaw' sparring-partners had been imported to portray Warnock, who, you will remember, was himself a wrong-way rounder. Tut Whalley and Jim McAloon, a useful local man, supplied this additional help, and Benny showed up so well in training bouts with them that the experts were unanimous in their opinion that Lynch would easily reverse the previous decision.

With a view to making it easier for the Board of Control to rescind their ruling, the agreed conditions for the match were that it should be fought over fifteen rounds at eight stone—in other words that championship conditions would be in force.

At the beginning of May came the disclosure that the venue would be Parkhead and the date June 2nd. Dingley had his Lynch v. Warnock advertising posters printed and displayed with this spicy build-up : "Under championship conditions and for the Flyweight Championships of the World and of Great Britain subject to final approval by the British Boxing Board of Control."

Then came the bombshell. It took the form of a definite pronouncement from the B.B.B. of C. that, under no circumstances, would its members recognise the Parkhead bout as involving either of Lynch's titles. Further, in accordance with a decision of the Board's Stewards arrived at at a special meeting, the contest must be fought at eight stone and four ounces, thus taking it outside championship requirements.

Sure an' 'bejanie 'twas the blackest of days for Ould Oireland, but Warnock and his followers were not the only ones to be disgusted.

57

Benny was disgusted too; so disgusted that he started off on a mammoth binging expedition. But when you drink you put on weight, so Glasgow's golden-boy found himself up against a second and most expensive antagonist—the scales.

CHAPTER SIX

TROUBLE, REPENTANCE, AND A
GOLDEN PURSE

QUITE a large number of the boys came over from
Belfast and the scene assumed an international
complexion at the weigh-in as the Irish brogue blended
with the 'Glesca' dialect.

Warnock was first on to the scales, and his poundage was announced as being eight stone exactly, or
dead on the flyweight limit.

Benny then stepped forward clad in shorts and
ring shoes.

"Better take the lot off," said Dingley with a trace
of anxiety in his voice.

"It will na' make any difference, anyway," replied
the apparently unconcerned Benny as he moved on to
the scales.

There was a gasp from the audience as the scales
went down with a bang and it became clear that
Lynch was nowhere near the stipulated weight. After
some argument he mounted the scales naked, and
an angry murmur sped through the crowd when the
news came that the world champion was six and three
quarter pounds overweight or, to put it another way,
that he scaled eight stone seven—a full pound over the

championship poundage for bantamweight! In addition to this, his period of loose living had removed that glossy sheen of fitness, which is the trademark of physical perfection, from his skin.

Now the Rules of Boxing call for a one o'clock weigh-in on the day of a fight, and in the event of a contestant coming in overweight he is allowed an hour's grace in which to remove the surplus flesh. But obviously it was useless for Benny so much as to try, instead he quite cheerfully announced that he would pay the £150 forfeit money stipulated in the contracts, this to be deducted from his purse.

In spite of all the controversial happenings the fight was still a 'natural,' and though the night was cold with the threat of rain it did not damp the ardour of 20,000 fans who had the turnstiles clicking merrily and the refreshment bars doing a roaring trade.

No sooner had Lynch and Warnock entered the ring than it started to pelt with rain, but the Scot did his level best to get his friends home early when, with the very first punches of the fight, he nailed the Irishman with a left hook and right cross to the jaw, to send him hurtling half through the ropes. As Jimmy went down, many ringsiders nodded and glanced at each other knowingly. This, they construed, was going to be easy.

But was it? No one could concede weight to a fit Lynch, to a Lynch at his best, but though Warnock was giving away far more poundage than had any previous opponent of the Scot, the fact was that those surplus pounds which Benny carried that night consisted only of superflous flesh.

I suspect that he was bent on finishing it quickly, because he knew full well that the poison was back in his system, and had grave doubts as to whether, in that sort of condition, he would be able to travel the full journey at top speed.

Anyhow, Warnock rose to bob and weave his way out of trouble for the remainder of the round. He shaped better in the second, repeatedly getting home with straight right leads followed by an occasional left cross. Benny was not doing much, but it seemed that he was trying to get the hang of the Irish boxer's right leads with a view to whipping over his own right in the form of a cross-counter.

But it was no go, for Warnock's tip-and-run raids were executed with just a little too much alacrity for the sluggish Lynch. So things continued throughout the third; it being a clear case of a good boxer trained to razor-edged sharpness against a brilliant boxer who was way out of condition.

Perhaps Jimmy sensed his advantage and got a trifle over-confident—who knows—but he was shaken by a right uppercut in the fourth, and then Benny, darting in, dropped his rival with a barrage of lefts and rights in combination form. Before referee Arthur Myers could start counting, however, Warnock was back on his feet and mixing it lustily with his opponent. Even so it was the world champion's round.

The fifth was Warnock's, but the next three went to Lynch which, on my marking, meant that with the half-way mark gone Benny was just a shade ahead. Actually that eighth stanza was his best of the whole battle, for Warnock was in dire trouble on two occasions as a result of body bombardments. At one stage it looked as though he must cave in under the onslaught, but by dint of clever footwork and ringcraft Jimmy managed to extricate himself from being pinned in a corner and returned to the comparative safety of the centre of the ring.

Full of spunk, the Belfast warrior then proceeded to win the next five rounds in a row. By the twelfth, it was noticeable that in the close quarter exchanges—and, in the main, at long range as well—Warnock no longer found it necessary to back away when under fire. If anything, he now seemed to be the stronger of the two, though by the end of the thirteenth they were both showing marked signs of weariness.

Benny presumably realised that he had dropped behind, because he rallied grimly in the fourteenth, though the old pith and snap were missing. Warnock was getting aggressive on his own account by this time, and they slugged it out determinedly in mid-ring, neither being willing to give ground. Pulling out an old trick, Lynch backed away, then jumped back in to catch Jimmy with a smashing right hook to the jaw. It must have been heartbreaking for the champion to see Warnock take it without flinching. Again and again Benny tried to find the range with his heavy artillery, but he was slow and the clever ducking and smothering of the southpaw Irishman made him miss and flounder about badly.

Excitement reached fever pitch as they came up for the last round. Few fight-fans keep a round by round tally, and the general view seemed to be that this was a real close one and this stanza could sway the issue either way. Lynch bored in to pummel his man about the body with short, two-handed bursts, though it couldn't have been a very pleasant experience to find his adversary absorbing them without noticeable effect, for Benny was putting everything he had behind every blow.

Dancing clear, Warnock contrived to make the issue a long-range one for a time, scoring freely with his leads to the head. This didn't suit Benny, who charged in, head down. It was all or nothing now, so the Irish contender stood his ground and traded punches with the champion, and they thumped away at each other with complete abandon but little effect until the bell.

Though Benny had probably shaded both the fourteenth and the final session, he hadn't succeeded in making up the leeway and Mr. Myers, after consulting his scorecard amidst a tense hush, walked across to Warnock's corner and raised his arm aloft. Benny looked bewildered, for he thought he had done enough to win, and at once all hell was let loose outside the ring.

With two victories under his belt against the world champion, what price Jimmy Warnock in a third attempt with the titles at stake? For the Irish larruper, it will be recalled, was still the leading contender, and now had only to beat wide-eyed Peter Kane (who had already eliminated Phil Milligan) to qualify as official challenger. But Jimmy and Benny were not destined to meet again, for in the final eliminator Warnock was knocked out in the fourth round by the Golborne Blacksmith who had once acted as Benny's sparring-partner.

It was but natural that, after losing a second time

to Warnock, Lynch should come in for a great deal of criticism, and soon the whispers began to circulate that: "Lynch is finished; he's all sold out. Doesn't try to get fit. Fed up with the game. He's lost his big dig."

These malicious rumours spread as far south as the headquarters of the Board of Control in London, and Benny was invited down and asked to explain his sudden weight increase before and lack of condition on the day of the Warnock fight.

It was pointed out to him that he would soon be called on to defend his World and British titles against Kane. It was carefully explained to him how important it is that the conduct of a champion should at all times be above reproach. How he should be an example to the multitudes who hero-worshipped him; male and female, young and old alike.

Lovable Benny took it all in and was truly repentant. He was sorry. He would mend his ways. Nobody, and I mean nobody, could have been more sincere in what they said.

So far, so good. And the pessimistic gentlemen who thought that Lynch was finished were quite wrong. In fact, for me and a whole host of others, Benny's finest hour was still to come, but I shall be devoting the succeeding chapter to that.

Immediately he got back to Scotland Benny went into strict training. He was back on course, and he meant to prove it to the world in general and to himself in particular.

To this end he agreed to meet an Australian named Roy Underwood on August 20th. Underwood had no

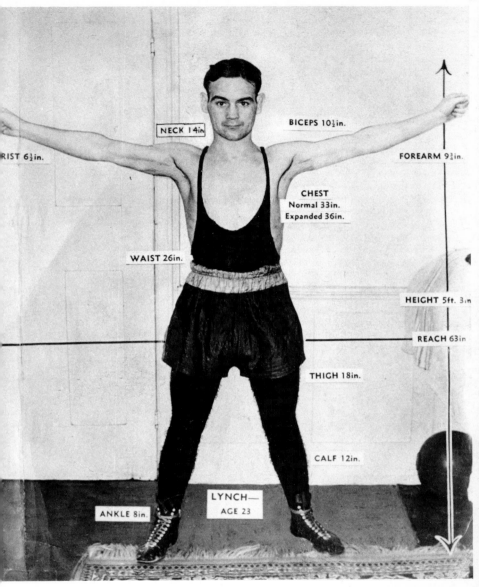

Showing the exact measurements of the wonderful little Scot who conquered the world. *(Scotsman Publications Ltd)*

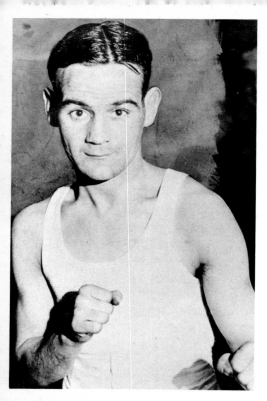

Benny in his prime.
(Scotsman Publications Ltd)

Lynch annihilates Manchester's Jackie Brown to win the world title on 9 September 1935.
(Scotsman Publications Ltd)

real pretensions to being ranked in the same class as
Lynch, but the fact that the match was made at eight
stone one — and that Benny came in at the agreed
weight — gave the bout a certain importance which
it would otherwise have lacked.

It went on at Shawfield Park and its outcome
was to put Benny back in the headlines for, after
giving a brilliant display of scientific boxing combined
with heavy hitting, the world champion battered the
lad from down under into submission inside six rounds.

You see, for months now the Scot had been boxing
at around the bantamweight limit, and with the title
defence against Peter Kane looming on the horizon this
impressive outing against Underwood near the championship poundage went a long way towards restoring
public confidence in Lynch's ability to make eight stone
and still be strong.

Nevertheless, a nagging doubt still lingered. The
champ was becoming unpredictable; if only one could
be sure. But Benny himself had no doubts whatsoever
and was completely untroubled at the prospect of putting his titles on the line. His confidence in his own
ability remained unshaken, and he hastened to assure
his friends that he'd "beat that Kane wi' nae bother
at a'!"

Naturally Scotland's 'Mister Boxing,' George
Dingley, was determined to secure the fight for Glasgow.
He knew he would be up against fierce opposition from
promoters all over the British Isles, but this did not
deter him. His great trump card was Lynch, who had
verbally promised his mentor that his next title defence

would be under his (Dingley's) promotion, and he relied upon Benny keeping his word.

But Liverpool held just as strong a hold on Kane. The promoter there made tempting offers to the Scot to defend his crowns on Peter's doorstep, but all in vain. In turn, Dingley found Kane just as diffident about travelling to Glasgow for the match. Meanwhile offers were coming in from big-time London impresarios, and something had to be done in a hurry if the match wasn't to be lost altogether.

First of all a contract was drawn up and signed by Lynch. This entitled him to 37½ per cent of the gate, an agreement which the canny champion found very satisfactory. He no doubt had in mind the thirty thousand odd spectators who had paid to see him defend his laurels against Pat Palmer, and it was more than likely that this number would be exceeded when he clashed with Kane.

Having settled half his troubles as he thought, Dingley made a surprise trip to Liverpool, saw Kane and came away with Peter's signature on a contract that guaranteed the nineteen year old fighter the sum of £1,500. Chuckling to himself, George tore home to get his arrangements under way, only to meet an unexpected hitch.

In his absence, a London promoter had wired a magnificent offer that made Benny want to change his mind. He asked Dingley to bite at the London bait, whereupon George promptly told the fighter he would guarantee him £4,000. Lynch accepted without hesitation and the big fight was on. Signed, sealed and settled for Shawfield Park on the night of October 13th.

CHAPTER SEVEN

THE FINEST HOUR AND ITS AFTERMATH

DIMLY, vaguely, Benny could remember the time when he didn't have a dozen suits; when a pound note was a lot of money and a promoter was the boss and therefore someone to be treated with respect. Not, of course, that he'd ever see those days again. It was all like a bad dream, like an ogre which could be produced to frighten a child.

But in many ways the world champion was still a child, and the sobering thought of what the loss of his titles would mean to him awakened that iron determination which had put him where he was. No more headlines, no more big purses, small print on the posters and finally, perhaps, oblivion.

For though he never entertained the thought of defeat, Benny knew only too well that an ex-champion is, well, just another fighter.

Training for the Kane fight was purgatory. This time it had to be eight stone . . . . or else! Lynch trained away from home at a place called Campsie, and there he waged his own private battle of the bulge as daily, clad in the long woollen training-suit and sweaters which had provided a labour of love for Granny

Donnelly and her knitting needles, he sweated to keep his weight down.

As fight-day approached, so Benny approached peak condition. By the day itself he had achieved razor-edged sharpness, was snapping at his manager like an irate terrier, being short-tempered with his friends and generally making it plain that he was in the sort of shape which fighters can only hold on to for at most a single day.

No flyweight pairing had aroused so much interest since the days of Jimmy Wilde. Everyone recognised in Lynch a champion in every sense of the word, a brilliant boxer, a cool tactician and a deadly puncher.

On the other hand, Peter Kane was a colourful performer whose ring personality appealed strongly to fight enthusiasts. Up on his toes, speedy and enterprising, the personification of perpetual motion, he was a joy to behold as he went hell-for-leather into his opponents in a non-stop effort to land a punch that would bring the bout to a summary conclusion. Unbeaten in the ring, he had won 33 of his 41 bouts inside the distance— a truly amazing record. In addition, he was entirely without fear and possessed the supreme confidence of youth in his abilities.

Many wondered if it was wise to match a lad of nineteen against a great champion, five years his senior. Benny, remember, had now been earning his living with his fists for more than seven years; Kane's experience was limited to less than three. Any such counsel was submerged beneath the clamourings of the majority who insisted that a contest between the pair was inevitable. The Golborne lad was a phenomenon and to deny him his chance could not be countenanced. This was a match that made itself—a 'natural,' as boxing folk say — and no one doubted that an epic struggle would result when Lynch and his youthful challenger crossed gloves in fistic combat.

In every boxer's career you can usually point a finger at one specific fight and say that this was the highlight of his record. Occasionally two men reach their peak on the same night, and then you see a truly memorable match. In my opinion that is what occurred on that October evening in Glasgow, and certainly neither man was ever quite so good again. In fact, many people claim that this was the greatest contest ever fought between flyweights.

As a financial proposition Lynch versus Kane was an assured winner from the start but, even so, no one could have visualised the startling scenes that occurred on the day. Forty thousand fans made their way to Shawfield Park that evening and, in spite of the fact that every precaution was taken for dealing with a large crowd, chaos reigned at the gates and more than once it looked as though ugly scenes would develop.

For some unknown reason there seemed to be only one entrance to the huge open-air arena, and it took an hour or so to get into the ground.

I shall not forget the behaviour of a Frenchman whom I watched perform outside. There were a lot of mounted and foot policemen, and I must say that for once a visitor did not think that 'our policemen are wonderful.' He had a certain amount of justification, for the mounted men were charging up and down the approaches to Shawfield as though they were taking part in a cavalry battle. The final straw, for this Gaul, came when a large Scottish policeman alleged that he had gone out of his turn in the queue and tried to make him go back about half-a-mile.

My own impression was that neither of them could understand a word the other was saying, but to my amazement I suddenly saw the policeman knocked stone-cold with a Carpentier-like right-hander and the excited Frenchman happily rubbing his hands in high glee.

He kept shouting: "Me, I just do not like ze policeman;" which was apparently justification enough, to his logical French mind, for having evinced his loathing and disgust in an international language far more expressive than Esperanto.

When his Scottish companions tried to remonstrate with him and to explain feverishly that this was no way to influence people and win friends in Britain they were met with the bland statement:

"Ah! You British are so hypocritical. You do not like ze policeman, I do not like ze policeman, NOBODY likes ze policeman. But when I demonstrate how I do not like ze policeman you make ze big fuss. Perfidious Albion!"

It was certainly a good build-up for the forthcoming battle, but I have never been more glad to get to my seat.

Long before the first bout was ready to go on it was plain to see that all records were going to be smashed. The crowd kept pouring in, and many of the ringside ticket-holders must have had grave doubts as to whether they would ever reach their seats in safety.

But Dingley's staff organisation withstood the onslaught, and after the fight it was established that over 43,000 people had managed to get into the arena, gate receipts totalling more than £12,500. And what a fight they saw!

Owing to the tremendous suppressed excitement of the vast crowd, the atmosphere was as though charged with electricity as referee W. Barrington Dalby—famous today as the B.B.C.'s number one inter-round summariser on Sound Radio—called both boxers and their chief seconds to the centre of the ring to issue his final instructions. A great hush descended like the sudden stopping of a powerful dynamo; then came the shrill clang of the gong and the fight was on.

And straightaway a sensation! In those days Kane was liable to win a fight with the very first punch, prancing out of his corner and nailing his man almost before the luckless opponent realised that hostilities had begun.

He tried to do it on this occasion, but Benny was ready for him, and there was a mighty roar from the crowd, invisible but tumultuously audible in the dark sea surrounding the bright island of the ring, when a left hook to the solar plexus and a vicious right to the jaw from the champion put Peter down for 'two.'

These were magnificent punches, and Kane went slithering back into the ropes before sinking into a sitting position. When he rose he was a most surprised and dazed looking lad, and he had already revealed his comparative rawness, firstly by being trapped by such a speedy attack and, secondly, in jumping to his feet so quickly.

Because he took such a short count and because he rallied so quickly and strongly, nobody thought that Kane had been seriously hurt by those blows. But if the truth is known the young blacksmith knew little about the fight after that first-round knockdown. In fact, although he fought back at Lynch, administered terrific punishment and took even more in return, Peter had no detailed recollection of what happened in the succeeding twelve rounds.

His former manager has since stated that, in the interval between the seventh and eighth rounds, the pop-eyed little man stiffened on his stool and enquired: "What round's coming up?" When he was told the eighth he looked unbelieving, for he remembered nothing of the subsequent twenty minutes odd fighting after Lynch delivered those first two devastating blows.

But you could never have guessed that from the exchanges themselves. For the first four rounds Peter did almost all the attacking, concentrating on blows to the ribs and under the heart while Benny, the better boxer, contented himself with countering to the head.

The challenger did his utmost to bring Lynch to the boards in the second, and he almost succeeded when a right, a fraction too high to take full effect, shook the champion to his toes. Both boys were punching pounds above their weight, standing close in and exchanging fierce blows in rapid succession. But although neither spared the other, there was no lack of true sportsmanship between them. Once Kane slipped to the canvas and Lynch immediately stepped back and allowed him to rise unhindered.

I made Kane fractionally ahead at the start of

the fifth, but suddenly Lynch began boxing with what seemed almost supernatural anticipation and icy calmness. Now he was content to let his challenger expend his energy, and at the same time wear him down and weaken him with vicious shots picked to strike home at vulnerable places. Sometimes he would back away under the very fury of Kane's dynamo-like punching, but the student of boxing—if he could have retained his coolness of perception—might have noticed that the champion was generally seeking and obtaining the inside position, thus enabling his blows to be the more crisply delivered.

After the fight had gone half its scheduled course, I made it level pegging, but the ninth found the Golborne blacksmith tiring rapidly. Then Lynch gave him a boxing lesson. He used his left, which he stuck out as rigid as an iron-bar, to keep Kane from getting to close quarters, but the challenger fought back with even greater determination.

Much of Peter's punching was wild, however, whereas Lynch was meticulously accurate with his deliveries and hurt his opponent whenever and wherever he landed. Kane looked as though he would be chopped down at any moment, yet this astonishing scrapper staged a fine rally just before the bell and, after pounding away fiercely to the body with both hands, suddenly switched to the jaw and staggered the titleholder with a tremendous right.

Encouraged by this, Kane made another desperate attack in the tenth session, chasing after his rival and hitting out strongly with either hand. Benny kept cool, however—perhaps he was deliberately biding his time—but

73

again he was given plenty to think about in the eleventh. Yet Lynch knew what he was doing, as the twelfth stanza was to show.

At the start it did not seem as though either man would have enough steam behind his punches to land the blow which would save the referee the trouble of adding up his points. Appearances proved deceptive, for soon Kane struck one of the hardest blows of the the fight, a left hook rather high on the champion's cheek.

As Peter leapt in to follow up his advantage, Lynch met him with a perfectly-timed left hook of his own, to the power of which was added the full weight of the challenger as he jumped forward.

Kane slipped to his knees, and although, once more, he stayed down for only two seconds he looked badly dazed when he rose. The green light was on for Benny, and the crowd sensed the 'kill.' Punch drunk and with fogged brain, bleeding from the nose and mouth, Kane simply refused to be finished off. He was driven pell-mell round the ring, and a hail of blows from Lynch added to gallant Peter's distress, which was palpable as he wobbled to his corner for the minute's rest.

Even now there was no thought of quitting. Kane toed the line for the thirteenth, but Lynch was far too good a tactician not to know when he had a fight won. He charged across the ring and swept his glassy-eyed and weakening rival back to the ropes with a fusillade of brain-curdling punches to the head.

Cold and merciless, Benny brushed aside the now feeble efforts of the adversary who had kept him at bay for so long. Now he would not be denied, and a left hook to the point of Peter's chin caused him to collapse over the bottom rope as if his legs had been filleted, his huge eyes rolling in pain and his mouth wide open.

The count had reached 'seven' before Kane achieved the seemingly impossible by dragging himself to his feet, but he was only postponing the inevitable. Lynch was the coolest man in the place. He picked his punches perfectly, and after another hooked barrage Kane went down again, his back toward the centre of the ring, his head bowed, and his body once more lolling over the bottom rope.

Peter made no move as Barrington Dalby screamed the count into his ear and banged on the canvas with his fist in an effort to make the prostrate fighter hear above the interminable din that was going on around the ringside. The valiant challenger was counted out there on one knee.

Usually any connection between the remarks boxers are alleged to make before or after fights have only a purely coincidental relationship with the truth or with real life, but Kane's truthful and modest: "All I can say is that I was well beaten by Lynch;" and Benny's intelligent summing-up: "I had the measure of him after the eighth round and I knew then that I would eventually knock him out. Kane was very very game;" were a verbal liqueur to the boxing banquet they had served up.

Well, Benny had proved his point. He still had his cherished championships and, though he had had to go through a hell on earth to do so, he had made eight stone and, not only that, he had put up the performance of his fighting life after having done it.

Champions who come in overweight for title defences forfeit their laurels on the scales, but that wasn't for Benny Lynch. He could always sweat it out and rise to the occasion when the chips were down. I honestly believe he thought that no one and nothing could ever deprive him of his world title.

Anyhow, with Peter Kane well and truly disposed of, the Scot was now freed for a time from that overhanging shadow of weight trouble. It was only appropriate that there should be a series of big celebrations, and the order of the day became eat, drink and be merry.

I'm sure if you'll bear in mind the conditions of dreadful poverty in which wee Benny had spent the larger part of his life you'll be able to understand why the adulation of the crowd should prove too heady a draught for this wonderful fighter to assimilate. Added to which those who knew him best tell me that Lynch had a horror of being considered 'high hat' by his friends, once he became a notable personality.

There can be no doubt whatsoever that many of his acquaintances battened outrageously on a champion's generosity, and for reasons of personal gain tempted him to indulge in those excesses which were to bring about his downfall.

Now read of the decline and fall, but, I pray, don't be too harsh in your judgment of this man who fought to live and lived to fight.

CHAPTER EIGHT

THE BATTLE OF THE BULGE — PART II

BENNY was drinking heavily and spending money fast. Funds were running low and something had to be dcne about it, so in mid-December the Glaswegian journeyed to Leicester where he was fixed to meet Georges Bataille, the bantamweight champion of France, over twelve rounds at eight stone six.

Though he came to our shores with a big reputation, the Frenchman did not measure up to the standard set by even a half-fit and grossly overweight Lynch, and he succumbed to the numbing punching of the Scot, the referee stopping the contest in Lynch's favour midway through the eighth round after Bataille had taken two long counts.

Maybe that result would appear to acquit Benny partially, yet it was badly marred by the fact that he could not even make this higher poundage without severe effort and came in at eight stone nine. Yet this was only two months after the successful defence of his titles against Kane.

Benny was certainly growing, but growing in the wrong places. There was a tyre of fat round his waistline, and he looked a good deal broader in the beam when he sat down.

That win over Bataille helps to show how easily things came to Lynch. Perhaps that was a reason for his ultimate downfall. He had no real need of hard training except to make weight, and required no lengthy sessions of gym work to perfect a new weapon. And I maintain that it was largely those prospects of an easy life that brought a brilliant boxing career to a premature end.

So ended 1937 and a year of mixed fortunes. On the credit side two great title defences against Small Montana and Peter Kane; on the debit side that disqualification against Len Hampston and the points loss to Jimmy Warnock.

What did the New Year hold in store for Benny? The lot. From the top of the heap to the end of the trail. From being a splendid fighter full of virility to entering the ring a lurching wreck loaded with alcohol. The sands were running out for Benny the world-beater.

Yet, with the perversity of fate, his first bout of 1938 turned out to be one of the easiest of his entire career. Before his 'ain folk' in Kelvin Hall Benny showed flashes of his best form when he battered Maurice Filhol from Paris into utter helplessness in five rounds, the referee applying the closure. And Filhol scarcely laid a glove on him the whole time!

Quite naturally, in view of their epic first struggle, Peter Kane was after a return with Lynch for the titles. His connections stated that they were willing to put up a £2,000 sidestake on behalf of their man, and so loud and insistent were their challenges that it became impossible to turn a deaf ear.

Dingley, negotiating on behalf of the world champion, claimed that Lynch was perfectly ready and willing to give Kane a second chance but, stalling for time, he added that Benny had already convincingly licked the Golborne lad and that there were other contenders who should now precede Peter in the quest for a title fight.

Eventually, after much discussion, it was agreed that Lynch and Kane should clash for a second time, but that the match should be an overweight one, though, in the event of Kane emerging as victor, he would be given another crack at Lynch's championships without further ado.

This time the Liverpool promoter, the late Johnny Best senior, secured the match for Anfield, Liverpool, on March 24th. There was a certain amount of give and take here, for the Lynch camp agreed to box in Kane's backyard only on condition that Peter's connections met their champion in the all-important matters of weight and distance. Benny's demand was for twelve rounds at eight stone six, and though this was finally agreed, Kane, who could do eight stone with ease, was vehement in his claim that eight stone three would have been a much fairer stipulation.

Be that as it may, Benny continued with his fast drinking right up to the day of the fight. He'd beat the very life out of that Kane this time, so that Peter would never have any inclination to share the same ring with him again.

You'd have thought that six full pounds over the odds would have been a comfortable enough weight allowance for any world flyweight champion about to engage in an important non-title bout—but no. For at the weigh-in a belligerent Benny came in one pound seven ounces overweight and, when he was told to sweat it out within the hour, became highly indignant and instructed his manager to write out a cheque for the £100 forfeit money involved forthwith.

It was the eve of the Grand National, and it was far from being an ideal night for an open-air show. A cold drizzle of rain descended on the stadium before the main event, a circumstance which contributed indirectly to the first sensation of the evening.

In view of the damp and chilling conditions, that famous referee, Mr. C. H. 'Pickles' Douglas, decided to give the boxers their final instructions in the dressing-room and to have them gloved up there.

No sooner had they been introduced after entering the ring than he instructed them to 'Box On,' whereupon both went into action vigorously without first observing the formality of shaking hands.

Like so many repeat performances of wonderful fights, this one was only a utility version of their former encounter, and in my opinion Benny was somewhat fortunate to share the honours of a draw. However, it is some indication of the calibre and genius of the man that he could so much as run a magnificent ringster like Kane close when he himself was only half-trained.

It was a hard but not a great fight, for it lacked one essential ingredient to raise it to the latter class—incident. There was not a single knockdown, though each fighter was staggered several times, and while each round was contested at well above average speed they lacked the touch of sheer fistic brilliance which had been present at the first meeting.

The second and only other sensation of the proceedings came when Mr. Douglas signalled a drawn verdict. The announcement met with abuse all round, the Liverpool 'skouses,' present in their thousands, booing and cat-calling their opinion that Kane had been hard done-by. Needless to say the Scottish element in the audience were equally vocal in championing the cause of their Benny.

Certainly a draw is something of a novelty in such an important bout as was this, but it was so close that, just for the record, I will give my own reading of the fight. I made Kane the winner by the narrow margin of six rounds against Lynch's four with two being even, or, in overall points tally, Kane the winner with a total of 59 points as against Benny's $58\frac{1}{2}$.

But let me hasten to add that, when things are as close as this, one should not adamantly disagree with the referee. After all, he is the only man actually in there with the boxers, and so is in a position to see more than anyone seated outside the ring—however knowledgeable they may be concerning the finer points of the game.

The Lancashire lad, I thought, took the first two rounds. Lynch tried to tag him early as he did at Glasgow, but this time the result was somewhat different. Blocking the left to the body and cleverly slipping the following right aimed at his jaw, the Golborne boy carried the fight to the champion, shaking him with a well-timed right which got home on the neck.

Benny went into a clinch, but as they broke Kane

81

hung another hard right plumb on his jaw and again
the Scot dived for shelter. He tried to steal the initiative
with hooked attacks, but Kane was a fraction too fast
on his feet and nimbly danced out of distance.

Feinting with his left in the second, Peter danced
in and, putting everything he had behind a right hook,
sent Lynch hurtling back into the ropes. Pandemonium
reigned as Kane went after his man two-fisted and with
grim intent. Benny was completely out of his depth. His
guarding of punches was faulty, and many of his best
blows were going astray.

The third was Lynch's and Kane, forced on the
defensive, had to be content with hit-and-run raids.
Benny was improving for, after sharing the fourth, he
won the fifth and sixth. Boxing now like the champion
he was, the Scot had Kane noticeably rattled. He was
picking Peter's punches off in mid-air and at the same
time doing fine work with his own left.

In an attempt to make his rival drop his arms
Kane went for the body. But his blows were right
on the border line, and twice Mr. Douglas warned
him to 'keep 'em up.'

A change came over the battle during the seventh,
and from this point on I could only credit Lynch
with taking the honours in the final round. The seventh,
eighth, tenth and eleventh I marked down to Kane,
with the ninth even.

Peter dished out plenty of punishment in the seventh, and only the fact that Lynch's greater experience
enabled him to tie his younger rival up at close quarters
saved him from being in serious trouble.

So the ex-blacksmith stayed at long range in the

eighth and found it paid dividends. Lynch was content to stall around and wait for an opening, but on the few occasions when he did throw his famed left hook he was hopelessly out of distance and finished off-balance. Kane was given plenty of time to pick his spot before countering heavily.

The eleventh was a bad round for Benny, his worst of the fight. First he walked right on to a righthander to the nose which shook him up badly. Urged on by the roar of the crowd, Kane charged in to finish the job and the world champion's legs turned to putty. It looked like the pay-off.

But wait! Suddenly Lynch was fighting back and, though he was still groggy, the fighting brain of a ringmaster helped him to punch, smother and stall alternately to stay on his feet until the bell.

Summoning a reserve of stamina from goodness knows where, Benny came back to win the closer. Did Kane help him do it? Just three seconds after they'd touched gloves he had the world champion reeling under combination punches, and then Benny went fighting mad.

He went tearing after Kane, tossing his old left hook equaliser with complete abandon. Often he missed, but sometimes he connected. Yet something had gone wrong, for Peter was taking it and coming back for more. The viper had lost its sting. Benny was disarmed.

Even so, he discarded any semblance of defence and kept crowding in, tossing leather all the time. It ended with Benny and Peter slugging it out relentlessly in the centre of the ring. A draw.

Kane was philosophic about it all. "I thought I had won," he said, "but I suppose the ref. knows best."

Benny thought a draw was "just right." Of his opponent he said : "Kane has improved tremendously since our first meeting—and he was a wonderful fighter then!" On the subject of a proposed third match with his titles at stake the world champion declaimed : " 'Course I'll gie him his chance, but they tell me I've tae tak' on some Yank first."

Unfortunately, Lynch had by now embarked on a private life which earned him the most stringent criticism of his true friends. It was well-known in boxing circles that Benny was prepared to pay forfeit when engaged in a non-title fight at a stipulated poundage sooner than burden himself with the rigours of training.

This caused great worry both to his manager and to the promoters who utilised his services, and the bad publicity he received on this account after the second Kane affair had a very adverse effect on his popularity.

Yet, even at this stage, the most discerning judge could not have foreseen what the future held for Benny Lynch . . . .

CHAPTER NINE

EX-CHAMPION EVEN TO HIMSELF

T ROUBLES never come singly. Benny Lynch could have testified to the truth of that old saying, for by the end of April he was up to his ears in trouble. Since his last fight his riotous behaviour had lost him a great deal of prestige and, moreover, the Board of Control was now taking an active interest in the world champion's affairs. In view of Benny's serious lapses in the matter of his weight, the Stewards had demanded a deposit of £500 as a safeguard against future offences.

Added to this, what with going off on wild sprees with a gang of cronies, making bad investments, being 'tapped' right, left and centre, together with playing the dogs and gee-gees, Lynch was distinctly short of cash. He drowned his sorrows only to find that this procedure made the hole in his pocket even bigger.

And now, to crown it all, he was called on to defend his world title. The nominated opponent was Jackie Jurich who hailed from sunny California, a youngster of twenty whom the Americans had unearthed, after scouring their vast continent, in an attempt to find a flyweight challenger capable of annexing Lynch's championship and taking it back to the States.

George Dingley immediately contacted Jurich's manager, Johnny Rogers, and terms were agreed for the fight to be held at the end of June on the ground of the St. Mirren football club at Love Street, Paisley.

So Jackie and his mentors set forth on their 7,000-mile journey, and unwittingly set in motion the mills of the Gods which were to transform Lynch from being the idol of the mob into an abject figure of scorn and derision. Retribution was at hand. The dark days had come.

"If you promise me faithfully that you'll come in at the flyweight limit, I'll give you £1,000 of your purse in advance to help you out," Dingley told Benny. "But are you quite sure you really can do eight stone?"

"We've taken the match and I'll make the weight just like I've always done for title fights," replied Benny. "Now dinna ye worry aboot a thing."

But it must have been obvious to the majority of boxing fans the world over that Lynch was now embarking on the most gruelling trial of his career. I was still a schoolboy at the time, but even I knew it. For since he had last defended his laurels some eight months previously, the champion had not even come in at the bantamweight poundage.

Though his everyday weight was now around eight stone ten, there are none so blind as those who do not wish to see, and certainly the Scots had a blind faith in their champion. He'd rise to the occasion again, you'd see. Do the double, too, by making the weight and winning.

On the Sunday before the fight a large and curious throng trekked to Campsie to watch one of Benny's training sessions. With meticulous thoroughness, he was hard at it in the hot sunshine, clad in heavy woollens and a sweat-suit. The eyebrows were well down, but the expression which used to portray only grim determination that day conveyed some new emotion. Was it anxiety? Perhaps desperation? Or even despair?

Trainer 'Puggy' Morgan's poker-face conveyed — absolutely nothing. George Dingley's expression, too, was inscrutable, but at least he showed no trace of anxiety whatsoever. Everything was apparently under control.

Back to Benny. He was moving nicely, hitting powerfully and his timing was just right. True, it was obvious that he still had some weight to shed, but then he still had three days to go and the drying-out process (fighters desperately tight for weight sometimes forego all fluids for forty-eight hours before a weigh-in) hadn't yet started. So, despite the rumours, Benny might make it after all.

Such was the consensus of opinion as the day of the fight dawned. Soon after midday a strangely subdued crowd gathered at Newspaper House, Glasgow, there to await the one o'clock weigh-in. It was in an atmosphere of tense but repressed excitment that zero hour approached. At the scales stood the late Charles Donmall, General Secretary of the B.B.B. of C., together with William Walker, chairman of the Scottish Area Council of that body.

The American was first to strip and weigh, and there was some polite clapping when it was announced that he was well inside the limit at seven stone twelve and a half. Then Benny mounted the scales.

You could have heard a pin drop as the officials carefully studied and adjusted the balance. After what seemed an age Mr. Donmall spoke.

"Step off," he said to Lynch. Then, turning to face the crowd, he announced impassively: "Lynch weighs eight stone six-and-a-half."

Instantly the place was in uproar as reporters dived for telephones to send the message which would make headline news. There could be no question of Benny trying to remove nearly half a stone in the one hour's grace allowed, and so the little Scot, who had taken so long and fought so hard to win the world championship, lost it in a miserable anti-climax before even entering the Paisley ring.

Soon word filtered through to the multitude waiting in the street outside the premises. The news spread like wildfire, and everywhere the cry was taken up. Complete strangers were stopped in the roads and informed that: "Wee Benny's thrown awa' his title. Couldna' even mak' bantamweight!"

In a nearby restaurant, with great tears rolling down his cheeks, Benny was forcing down his first solid meal in days. He kept repeating to his sad-faced handlers: "I did ma best; I really tried. I couldna' help it."

Back at Newspaper House Messrs. Donmall and Walker stood at the scales, maintaining their hopeless sixty minute vigil. According to the rules the world championship was still Benny's until two p.m., but the whole world knew by now that Lynch would never make eight-stone again. Scotland and Britain was about to lose her only world boxing title and, at one minute past the hour, the Flyweight Championship of the World was officially declared vacant.

Jackie Jurich, most naturally, was bitterly disappointed, but he sportingly agreed to go through with the bout in order that the spectators who had purchased tickets should be given a run for their money. He also picked up, through Lynch's default, the £500 deposit the latter had been made to lodge with the Board.

Stunned by the news, the man who, apart from Lynch, was most affected by it—George Dingley—sat in an ante-room at Newspaper House, his world in ruins at his feet. Fate had dealt poor George a double blow, for not only had the fighter he managed forfeited an intensely valuable championship but, in addition, as promoter of the show Dingley had to agree to completely new terms for Jurich before the American's mentors would agree to let him concede the huge disparity in weight.

It was in an atmosphere of intense hostility that Benny made his way to the ringside that night. Only a few months earlier the fans had fought for the honour of doing him homage, but now his erstwhile partisans booed him every step of the way down the aisle, and men stood on chairs so that they might hurl abuse and insults at their former idol.

Lynch was in disgrace. He had committed the unpardonable sin of growing-up for, though he had neglected his training on plenty of other occasions, this time he had worked conscientiously and was fully fit at the higher poundage.

If proof was needed that Benny had put his back into his training chores—and with the ugly mood of the crowd towards him, believe me it was—that proof was forthcoming for all to see once the bout got under way. For if ever Lynch rose to the occasion, it was against Jurich, when the man who was supposed to be a villain and to be finished turned in one of his most masterful displays to make the best that America could produce look like a novice.

What a man and what a fighter was this Lynch; a real-life Jekyll and Hyde if ever there was one! His first effort that sultry summer night was to acknowledge the hostile reception of his ex-supporters with as dignified a little bow as ever you saw, so perfectly executed that I'm sure it left the rowdies thoroughly ashamed of themselves.

Right from the off it was obvious that the Scot was an infinitely better fighter than Jurich could ever hope to be. So superb and effortless was Benny's display that many of the people who had booed and hissed him when he made his entry into the arena cheered him after the fight was over—completely won over by the excellence of his boxing artistry.

Jurich was good, very good, but just not good enough. For fleet-footed Jackie was up against an inspired rival who was superb. Benny floored him momentarily in the opening round with a left hook, then proceeded to 'carry' his man along as cleverly as ever he had done in his far-off booth days. I don't know why Benny did it, but I like to think that it was because he knew the people were disappointed at the forfeiture of Scotland's first-ever world title, and that he wanted to atone as far as possible by ensuring that

90

the audience saw a lengthy spectacle which they would not soon forget. As for me, I'll NEVER forget it.

Later in the bout Lynch twice helped his fallen opponent to rise, and time after time he stood off when Jurich stumbled or was stunned by heavy blows. Frequently he smiled when the Yank scored with a good blow.

True greatness in any sphere cannot be hidden, no matter how cleverly it may be disguised, and in spite of themselves, those who had come to sneer stood on their feet to cheer. Once again the old war-cry rang out: "Guid auld Benny boy!!!"

None of these things should be allowed to detract from the grand showing of Jurich, who was attempting the virtually impossible in giving away so many pounds. The American's display was a fine one against such odds, plus a fit Lynch, and his perseverance and gameness were worthy of the enthusiastic ovation accorded him.

But the dice was loaded too heavily in Benny's favour. If he wasn't quite as strong as he had been in his earlier big fights, this was only because of his weight-reducing efforts which, though they had failed, had sapped some of his vitality. Even so, the Glaswegian was a far more dangerous proposition against Jurich than he had been for some months past.

In the seventh round the foreigner was downed for 'eight,' and on rising he was immediately dropped again for a similar count. More heavy punishment came Jackie's way in the ninth, when he was twice felled for 'nine,' but still he resisted gallantly. Even when he was finally splayed on the canvas and counted out in the twelfth, the valiant Californian was striving

91

manfully to heave himself erect when the fatal 'ten' was tolled over him.

On his return to the dressing-room Benny must have pondered on the fickleness of fight-fans, for he had to force a passage through a wildly cheering mob who struggled frantically to shake his hand, pat him on the back or even to touch him. But the wee fellow from the Gorbals didn't resent it—far from it. Rather did he welcome such hero-worship, for it brought him a new glimmer of hope.

One thing stood out in Benny's mind. He might not be a world champion any more, but there was still a chance for him to reach the top among the bantamweights.

Of course, it wasn't as simple as that, for Benny had to account to the B.B.B. of C. for his latest offence, and disciplinary action was sure to be taken. He might even be deprived of his licence to box altogether or, nearly as bad, suspended indefinitely.

The Board, however, saw fit to temper their justice with mercy, and Lynch was permitted to continue boxing, subject to certain conditions. The first of these was that he must quit the flyweight division once and for all—which meant that he must relinquish the British title which he still held — secondly, his training and poundage must be open to constant checking by two officials of the Board, William Walker and Doctor Daniel Miller. Finally, a further £500 must be deposited at the Board's H.Q., to be automatically forfeited in the event of any future infringements.

Benny willingly and thankfully accepted these conditions. They gave him a chance to get back up there on his pedestal, and that meant everything to him. With this object in view, he set up new training quarters at Langholm, and engaged a new conditioner in the person of Johnny McMillan, a former featherweight champion of Scotland.

Arrangements were made for him to make his official debut as a fully-fledged bantam in a twelve-rounder at Shawfield Park on September 27th. To make things easier for Benny in the matter of weight, it was agreed that the fight would be fought at eight stone ten— which is actually half-way between bantamweight and the featherweight limit of nine stone.

Yet his opponent was to be anything but a set-up, for slated to occupy the opposite corner of the ring was none other than the colourful Kayo Morgan, a cigar-smoking 'southpaw' from Detroit. Kayo was a top-class performer as the Scots fans well knew, for on previous visits there he had lived up to his name by knocking out Johnny McGrory and Johnny McMillan. McMillan, now retired and training Lynch, let it be known that he had learnt a lot about Morgan, and that he would put Benny wise on how to beat him.

The American's latest triumph had been to thrash soundly the then reigning world bantamweight champion Sixto Escobar, and there was no doubt that if Benny could show up well against Morgan he must have a real chance of getting back to the top of the tree.

Loyal George Dingley was yet again the promoter, but back at Langholm something had gone radically wrong with the fighting machine that had been Benny

93

Lynch. Now he was fighting a losing battle against something much bigger than himself. No longer could he control his thirst and his ever-increasing weight. Together they had become the bugbear of his existence, and together they transformed his life into a cloak and dagger existence. He was fined £20 and had his licence disqualified for driving a car under the influence of drink.

Kilmarnock's Court Sheriff gave Benny good advice. "Cut out drink altogether . . . . boxing and the bottle, sport and spirits do not go together." Alas, his warning came several thousand drinks too late.

Benny's £500 deposit took wings when he tipped the beam for the Morgan fight at nine stone one pound fourteen ounces; nearly six pounds overweight.

Nevertheless, the fight itself kept that flicker of hope alive, for Kayo was made to travel the full distance before being awarded a hotly-disputed points decision. Most of those present felt that Lynch had done enough to win, or at least to earn a draw, for the Scot dictated the pattern of the fight from start to finish. Maybe he could still make the grade.

But it was not to be. His last fight on an advertised bill came when, early in October, Benny was brought to the Empress Hall, Earls Court (London), there to box Aurel Toma, a Roumanian who had once been ex-King Carol's chauffeur and was alleged to have taught ex-King Michael how to box. These were the premises of the National Sporting Club, and it was an opportunity for Benny to get back into favour if he could put on a good show for the members.

Toma had appeared several times in London and seemed unlikely to set either the Thames or the Empress

Hall on fire, but I must say he looked more the fighting man, with his glowing swarthy skin and his snapping black eyes, than the pasty-faced, tubby, old-young travesty of an athlete who faced him that night and who fought under the name of Benny Lynch.

When Benny arrived at the hall it was obvious to all who saw him that he was in no condition to box. At the weigh-in that day he had scaled nine stone five and a quarter against Toma's eight seven. The weight stipulation, originally eight-eight, had later been raised to eight-ten and finally to catchweights. Perhaps Toma's handlers realised that the heavier Lynch weighed, the less formidable would he be and the more easily would he succumb.

The sight—I cannot call it a fight—was so embarrassingly pitiful that I do not propose to dwell on it. Suffice it to say that Benny did not land a single clean or damaging blow, and that he scarcely bothered to defend himself against the Roumanian's 'feather-duster' punches. In the third round Lynch seemed to misjudge his distance from the ropes, fell back on to the canvas and remained there apparently half-asleep to be counted out. It was the only time he was ever knocked out in his life, and it came against a boxer whom he would unquestionably have out-classed had he been even remotely fit.

Again Lynch had the bitter experience of being execrated by the crowd. It was a pathetic sight as, with bowed head and looking at the ground, he was led away through the howling, jeering multitude. I can't believe that many of those present had been fortunate enough to witness Benny's blazing victories, for if they had surely they would merely have bowed their heads in silence at this pitiful tragedy of the ring.

Lynch had previously been examined by the doctor attached to the Club—in the same way as every boxer is examined before he is allowed to take the ring. But in this case Benny was subjected not to an ordinary physical examination but to a sobriety test. He was made to walk along a straight line, touch his nose with his eyes shut, and was put through all the other trials which are used in a police station when a man's sobriety is doubted.

Technically he was able to pass these, but it was obvious that he had been sobering up with caffeine tablets, and clearly he was not fighting fit. It was a pity that he was allowed to enter the ring, for after the travesty he frankly admitted that his weakness was alcohol, and in a Press interview he said: "My next fight will be with John Barleycorn."

It's good to be able to place on record the fact that there were still some people who had faith in Benny, faith in his ability to recapture his stature both as a fighter and as a man. Particularly good because the tragic boxer tried desperately to do both.

Among these people were the blue-blooded members of the National Sporting Club, an institution dedicated to furthering the cause of British sport in general and of British boxers and boxing in particular.

These gentlemen signified their intention of doing everything in their power to put the Scottish battler back where he belonged, and to remove the chip from his shoulder which grew bigger with every drink he took.

Match maker Len Harvey (seated) watches Benny signing contracts for the undisputed championship fight with Small Montana at Wembley Pool, 19 January 1937. Also shown are manager George Dingly and promoter Sidney Hulls.
(Tommy Edmond)

(Below left) Note the thickening features – Benny is running down hill *(Scotsman Publications Ltd)*. *(Below right)* A troubled Lynch shown after his sojourn at Chislehurst and before he left to stay in the Irish monastery.
(Tommy Edmond)

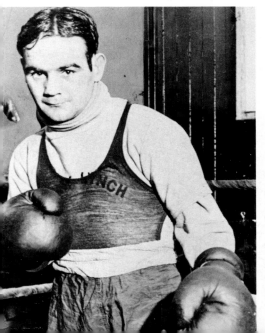

To
the Memory
of
BENNY LYNCH
UNDEFEATED FLYWEIGHT
CHAMPION OF THE WORLD.
THE FIRST SCOTSMAN TO WIN
A WORLD BOXING TITLE.
BORN 2ND APRIL 1913.
DIED 6TH AUGUST 1946.
HIS SON
JOHN JAMES
DIED 18TH DECEMBER 1970.
AGED 34 YEARS

ERECTED BY
BOXING FANS.

"ALWAYS A FIGHTER"

R.I.P

LYNCH

Life-long admirer Tommy Edmond tends the Wee Fellow's grave and lives with his memories. *(Scotsman Publications Ltd)*

To this end they were prepared to pay all expenses for Benny to take a long holiday in the country at a rest home and to follow it by going on a cruise. When the ex-champ. was fit again, they would sponsor his comeback campaign.

Benny expressed his thanks in the only way he knew how. With a promise to do his best, and the hope that he wouldn't let his benefactors down.

CHAPTER TEN

DRINK SEEMED THE ONLY SOLUTION

ON the way to the home in Chislehurst, Kent, where he was to undergo a cure for inebriates, Benny and the ever faithful Dingley, who was escorting him, called in at the Plaza Hotel, London, where they had a few words with close friends Moss Deyong and journalist John Macadam, together with a representative of the National Sporting Club.

Benny's blood-flecked eyes stared pleadingly from his pasty-face and he was bloated and shiny with whisky fat, but just as he was about to leave to catch the Kent-bound train he blurted out: "This is going to be the toughest fight of all. Please pray to God that I win."

That was in the late Autumn of 1938, and now we move on to mid-November of the same year.

Striding purposefully through the lanes around Chislehurst, Lynch sniffed at the invigorating air appreciatively. As the blood tingled through his veins a feeling of exultation surged through him. He was rising to the occasion like he always had. He'd got over the first three weeks of the cure without disaster and, though he'd had long hours of excruciating agony to endure, Benny had survived them and had got over

what the doctors had told him would be the most testing time. Right now he felt on top of the world.

But fate wasn't kind. Soon came a message from
home which was to have far-reaching effects. Benny's
son, John, was in hospital with a leg injury and had
taken a serious turn for the worse. It was feared that
the leg might have to be amputated.

At once all else was forgotten as Benny made
a hurried dash to Glasgow in order that he might be
at the bedside of his son. After a couple of days little
John's condition improved; the crisis passed and the
malignancy was dispersed. The boy was pronounced
'out of danger.'

Not so his Dad, for back home again he was
continually running into some of the old crowd who,
in spite of his protests that he was off the stuff, insisted
that he just have one for 'old time's sake.'

The temptation was too great. Nevertheless, probably because he had had little to drink for weeks, Benny
was very ill after one monumental session. This brought
him to his senses and, still resolute in his intention,
he caught a train back to Chislehurst.

Regrettably it was very different now. The peace
and quiet which the ex-world champion had found
soothing before now irritated him beyond measure. His
nerves were on edge and the long nights of wakeful-
ness became maddening as he paced the floor unceas-
ingly in an effort to induce sleep. Alas, it was no
use . . . .

Inside a week Benny had packed his bags and
returned to Glasgow. Not that he was giving up the

fight; it was just that he'd decided the venue should be his own backyard.

There were no cheering throngs to welcome him back this time, and he passed almost unnoticed down Sauchiehall Street in the Gorbals where once the taxi carrying him had been dragged by cheering fellow-countrymen. His arrival at the station was not quite unnoticed, however, for as Benny stepped to the platform a small group, headed by his wife, moved forward to greet him. There were still some who stood by him, and they had come to tell him so and to say 'Welcome Home.' True, they didn't cheer or wave flags, but their quiet greeting brought a lump to the throat of the prodigal.

Among them was Johnny McGrory, himself now an 'ex-champion.' Johnny, a young man of sterling character, had a special interest, for, since they'd been kids together at the St. John's Boys' Guild, he and Benny had climbed the fistic ladder together. A real bond of affection existed between the pair.

With wisdom beyond his years, McGrory realised that here in Glasgow, surrounded as he was bound to be by temptation, Benny would never survive. Johnny had come to plead with his pal to cut himself adrift from it all.

"But how?" asked Benny, for in his more lucid moments he was filled with remorse and was prepared to do anything which would purge him of the poison which was eating into his very soul.

Having obtained Lynch's word that he would be guided by his advice Johnny, a devout Roman Catholic, proceeded with his plans. A few days later Benny set

sail for Ireland, there to visit Mount Melleray Monastery, which is situated some 140 miles from Dublin, and
place himself in the care of Father Abbot. In that
atmosphere of quiet and spiritual tranquility he would
try to find peace and the strength to conquer his
weakness.

It was a losing battle. Instead of finding shelter
midst the calm of the simple life of the monks, Benny
found only the tortures of the damned as he waged
his fight against the devil that was within him. He was
home for Hogmanay, but broken in spirit and with
neither the strength nor desire to carry on.

Help was even now at hand, for the faithful little
band of followers steadfastly refused to abandon hope.
They were counting on the fighting spirit that had made
Benny one of the greatest boxers of his day.

Everything had been arranged, and for the first
stage of his recuperation Lynch was to stay with Granny
Donnelly in Orchard Street. Here he would be within
easy reach of 'the braes' where he had worn many a path
doing roadwork in the early days, and for sparring and
other work there were a host of small gymnasiums in
the district. With reasonable luck we'd see him back
in action yet!

Under Granny's eagle-eye the colour soon began
to return to Benny's cheeks, the sparkle to his eye and,
what's more, that nervy habit he had acquired of drum-
ming ceaselessly with his fingers and twitching his
shoulders had practically disappeared.

There was, of course, still the odd occasion when
Uncle Jimmy was called on to sit and talk with Benny
during a restless night, or to walk with him through

the deserted streets until an attack of the jitters had passed. But Uncle Jimmy's vigilance was being rewarded. There were no bottles concealed in secret hiding-places, and no furtive trips to the nearest boozer. Victory was just round the the corner, for Benny was well on the way to recovery.

For the last part of the cure, Lynch was transferred to the charge of one Tim McMahon. A staunch supporter of the Glaswegian since the early days, Tim's burning ambition now was to see the ex-champion back in the ring. To this end he placed at Benny's disposal a caravan situated on the lonely moors of Corbeth, in Dumbartonshire, about ten miles from the city.

To keep him company were featherweight Frank Kenny and his manager, Johnny Kelly, and in those ideal surroundings more progress was made, result of which was that the urge to make a comeback was reborn in Benny's heart.

Meanwhile Tim McMahon, hopeful of persuading George Dingley to fix a fight for Lynch on an open-air tournament at Parkhead, moved heaven and earth to bring this about but, alas, the whole show fell through. Finally, however, it was arranged that Benny should oppose a selected opponent down in Swansea.

Elated at the prospect of getting back into harness, he was doomed to disappointment. The bout was never to take place, for about this time the Scot figured in another incident that made front-page news and blasted for ever Benny's hopes of a comeback.

One night he disappeared from the caravan and, after a tremendous search of the moors by both police and civilians which lasted all night, Lynch was eventually found lying under a hedge. He was clad only in pyjamas and slippers and was suffering from exposure.

As so often before Benny was condemned without trial. It was the old, old story of 'give a dog a bad name . . '. People spoke of the orgies and goings-on which took place at these Lynch training-camps; stories which were the more dangerous because, in the past, there had sometimes been a fragment of truth to lend them weight. Yet this time they were nothing better than a complete fabrication of the truth.

What actually happened was that, in the pitch darkness, the little fellow tried to find his way to the lavatory which was some distance from the sleeping-quarters. To make matters worse there was a swirling mist and he went off at the wrong angle, so that when he tried to get back to the caravan he was again way out in his direction. Groping his way blindly about the moors, Benny finally sank to the ground, suffering from cold and exhaustion. It was there they found him next morning, and they were lucky to find him alive.

Why didn't he shout for help, you say? He was asked that by the police, and replied that he "didna' wanna' mak' a fuss." In any case, had he done so, the story would still have hit the headlines and as likely as not would have had the same outcome.

Which was that Benny's licence to box was withdrawn by the Board of Control, and so ended his attempt at a comeback. Keyed up as he had been, the disappointment proved too much. The only thing that had kept him going was no more. Benny Lynch was a 'has-been.'

What good to tell him that it was far better to be a 'has-been' than a 'never-was'? Next, he became that most unfortunate of all sporting figures, the ex-champion who can fight no more, has been trained for no job, and can only hang around the pubs getting free drinks on the strength of his past performances until even the bar-flies grow tired of the stories which he tells more and more confusedly.

From here on life did not have much to offer poor Lynch. He cut himself off from his old friends and sought forgetfulness in the gay life, but here, also, disillusionment was quickly forthcoming. Bereft of fame and glamour, Benny's sorties at the smart-set were met with aloofness and disdain on all sides. Now he was looked upon as just a drunken down-and-out and as a joke.

But those expensive tastes of his must needs be satisfied, and the forlorn figure was forced to swallow his pride and to pick up the scraps given as hospitality by his one-time 'equals.'

The freeze-out was gradual but effective, and those who had once crossed the street to greet him now did likewise to avoid him whenever he hove in sight. It was a bitter and lonely existence for one who, not so long ago, had been the toast of the town—nay, of the whole country. Only Benny was past caring. He had learned something of "Man's Inhumanity To Man," but the lesson had come too late.

So he moved to pastures new, to the small dimly-lit pubs and clubs where there were plenty of loafers who were prepared to listen to the meanderings of an ex-world champion. Though the social status was much lower than that to which Benny had been accustomed of late, he enjoyed the company, and the cheap flattery somehow helped to soothe the ache in his heart. But even in these joints one was expected to be in the chair once in a while, and lack of funds was becoming a serious problem with Lynch.

About this time his treasured collection of cups and trophies began to disappear from the house. Though their intrinsic value was perhaps not all that great, to Mrs. Lynch they were priceless heirlooms which would one day be handed down to their offspring.

Though Benny's fluctuating sense of values did not permit him to realise the gravity of the step which brought him his latest source of income, it was not without a pang of regret that he parted with his prizes, and it was typical of the man that on each occasion he returned with little token gifts for the family. It was his way of saying that he was sorry.

Try to understand that Lynch couldn't help himself; he just had to have money with which to purchase alcohol.

At first his wife was able to trace the trophies to various pawn-shops in the vicinity and redeem them. But it couldn't go on indefinitely, for as fast as they were replaced Benny made off with them again until finally all were gone. The last tangible evidence of a man's prowess scattered to the winds . . . .

I should be happy to end my story at that point, but I can't, for things were to get much worse. At home matters had reached a head, and Mrs. Lynch had been compelled to leave John with her mother and go out to work. This step had the effect of shocking

Benny into the realisation of his responsibilities, and he knew that something must be done—and quickly.

What could he do? In all his life Lynch had never held down a job for more than a few months, and he was unfitted for work simply because he'd never wanted to do any. The idea that one day he might have to earn a living with anything other than his fists had never even entered his head.

But the time had come for stern measures, so in tattered greatcoat, old cap and muffler, hands buried deep in his pockets Benny went out to see what he could find. It was a bad time he had chosen, for thousands of out-of-work shipyard hands were also engaged in the same pursuit.

Jobs were not easily picked up even by those who had the necessary qualifications and experience. Lynch's quest proved fruitless. Then came a day when Benny came home jauntily with a wide grin on his face. Everything was going to be all right. He had landed a job; a job he knew something about, too.

Know how he'd done it? Saw them erecting a boxing booth on a vacant site. Stood there watching glumly when he noticed the burly proprietor eyeing him askance. Suddenly Benny had a great idea.

"Can ye gie me a fight, mister?" Yes, the same words which, as we shall see, had first started the kid from the Gorbals along the knuckle trails that were to lead him to world fame—and back again to grinding poverty.

And when 'guvnor Tommy Woods heard who the

little unkempt man was, he straightaway invited him to travel with the show.

History was repeating itself. Benny was going back to the booths.

CHAPTER ELEVEN

THE LAST SAD CHAPTER OF ALL

H URRY, hurry, hurry along. You're still in capital time to see a genuine glove fight for a knockout featuring Benny Lynch, the former flyweight champion of the world. Great entertainment as suitable for ladies as for gentlemen so hurry, hurry, hurry!"

The 'barker' outside Tommy Woods' booth was making a colourful 'spiel' to make the throng who stood around the tent part with their sixpences. And why not? For once he really had something to shout about, for the travelling show possessed a super attraction.

It was the summer of 1939, and the holiday-makers in the north of Scotland, many of whom had for years worshipped Benny from afar, now had the opportunity of seeing him in action, and they were taking full advantage of the generous price of admission. Business was brisk, for Lynch could still draw like a mustard-plaster.

For the first time in many months the ex-champion knew a feeling bordering on contentment, for here in the booths he was wanted and was still a big-shot if only in a small way. Benny was well received, and a glow of satisfaction spread through him as he raised the shouts of the crowd.

What memories it must have awakened! Of golden rings at Shawfield Park, Belle Vue, Manchester, the Empire Pool, Wembley; the faces of his great opponents . . . and now the smoke and sawdust atmosphere of the fairground.

Life's a funny business, but providence makes us adaptable to its rapid changes, and probably Lynch now found that he derived as much pleasure from the cheers of this handful of people as ever he had on the big occasions.

For one thing the applause meant so much more to him now. It helped blot out the memory of that night at Earls Court when, as one newspaper put it, 'any connection between Lynch and a fighting man would have been a joke in poor taste.' It chased away the hollow feeling of despair. Perhaps the world was not such a bad place after all. These folk still admired him.

The booth fighters were real friends, too. Most of them Benny had known in the old days, and they hadn't changed a bit. Here he was just one of the boys, and as such came in for his share of horse-play and practical jokes which are part and parcel of life in a travelling show.

During working hours Benny took on all-comers and enjoyed every moment of it. At the offer of a pound to anyone who could stay three rounds there were plenty of outside takers who, even if they laid no claims to fistic prowess, were anxious to have a go so that they might claim the distinction of having crossed gloves with Benny Lynch. And, except when a 'fix' was specifically arranged, it was seldom that

Tommy Woods had to pay out, for though Benny was far from being in the best of condition, the craft still remained, while the old left hook, though not so fast or well concealed, was as devastating as ever.

Even when he took the ring with a deal of whisky and beer aboard, Benny was quite capable of taking care of those who cared to try their luck, no matter what their shape, size and weight.

But, with the end of the summer, came the end of the booth season, and Lynch found himself once more out of work. Now began a period of waiting and hoping, for Benny had applied for the reinstatement of his boxer's licence.

His application received prompt attention, and Benny was requested to submit himself to a special medical examination in London. Willingly he agreed, and on Monday, September 2nd, after a rigorous check-up, the two appointed Board doctors packed the Scot off home with the words: "O.K. Benny. We'll be letting you know."

Dark clouds of war were hanging over the Capital, and I suppose that the next day must have been one of the darkest of Benny's whole tragic life. He travelled back to Scotland through the night, and on alighting from the train at Glasgow Central made straight for the bookstall to buy the papers.

Imagine his horror when, splashed across the front page together with the crisis news, he saw: "Lynch comeback attempt refused. Board say not yet." There followed a formal B.B.B. of C. statement signed by the examining doctors to the effect that: "This is to certify that we have examined, this afternoon, Benjamin

Lynch, and in our opinion he is not at present fit to carry on his boxing career."

There was the proviso that he could continue training for a further three months, and then renew his application, but for Benny that proviso might never have existed.

When he got home there was a letter on the Board's notepaper which ran :— 'Dear Sir, With reference to your recent application for renewal of your Boxer's licence. This has now been considered, and it has been decided that the licence be not granted. Yours faithfully' . . . . The letter was signed by Charles Donmall in his capacity as General Secretary to the Board.

Within a matter of hours war had been declared, and the remnants of Benny's world lay scattered at his feet. He was sick of trying. His comeback was just a pipe-dream. No more would he struggle against the tide of misfortune; from here on he'd just drift and see where it took him. Besides, he reckoned he'd taken just about everything that could be dished out to him now, so things couldn't get much worse.

Despite his avowed intentions, Benny's better self make him attempt to enlist in the Services, within days of the outbreak of war. It was yet another disappointment when the doctor told him : "I'm afraid this is one fight you'll have to stay out of, Benny. But don't worry—there will be plenty of jobs at home for you which will be every bit as important."

He tried one or two of those jobs, such as the Home Guard and A.R.P. But none of them lasted long, for nowadays patience and regularity were not Benny's strong points. His system had long since been sapped of its power to create energy, he couldn't stand responsibility of any kind. Actually, his state of health was a good deal worse than he suspected.

Lynch soon found he was wrong in thinking that things couldn't get worse. They did get worse, much worse. Soon his wife left him and the home was broken up and sold. And who could blame her? The burden was too much.

There were rumours about at this time that Benny had once tried to do away with himself. Probably only the selflessness of his mother, who gave him refuge in her small house in the Paisley Road district, gave him strength to carry on. Though he had not known much home life in his early days, Benny found his mother eager to repair the deficiency, and the tragic figure of her son was made as comfortable as anyone could hope to be in a small tenement house in a narrow, dark street.

And so Benny drifted. A familiar figure stumbling around the streets of Glasgow, but a parody of his once sprightly self, he was now compelled to pay periodic visits to a hospital, where he learned the true state of the poll. This was that alcohol was slowly killing him, and that to continue drinking would be just another form of suicide. But this remained a secret which he shared with no one, as did the fact that he had contracted tuberculosis.

Still misfortune dogged the ex-boxer. His mother fell ill and died, so for the second time he was homeless. Yet though he knew that he would be welcomed by other relatives, the pride which had kept him aloof over the years would not permit him to climb down now. Benny intended to finish the course alone, and his new home was a working-men's lodging-house.

John Macadam, a friend of mine who was a close confidant of Lynch and who frequently warned him of the inevitable result attendant upon his way of life, tells a story of how Benny, whatever his faults may have been, to the end of his life maintained his generosity. Johnny McGrory, his old chum, had a benefit night during the war. An auction was held to help swell the funds and, from the back of the hall, stepped a short, fat man who looked ill and neglected. He held up a bundle to the auctioneer, saying: "Get what you can for this."

Then, without waiting for a word of thanks, he hurried back into the shadows. The auctioneer unwrapped the parcel. Inside he found a magnificent silk dressing-gown, and emblazoned across the back were the words: 'Benny Lynch, Flyweight Champion of the World.' It was Lynch's way of paying tribute to his friend.

I travelled up to Glasgow in June 1943 to see Jackie Paterson knock out Peter Kane for the flyweight title. On the same train were a number of newspaper men and dear old Moss Deyong, prince of referees. On emerging from the station and even before the porter following him with his bag could hail a cab, from somewhere near suddenly appeared a gross little barrel of a man, blubber-bellied and roll-necked, to inquire pleadingly of the famous referee:

"Have ye' got the price of a dinner, Mr. Deyong?" in that husky, drink-affected voice of his.

113

And Mossy, bless his heart, handed over a pound without so much as a murmur.

Off Benny went, as fast as his podgy, swollen legs would take him, to the nearest public house.

There was a similar incident in July 1946 when I went up to see Paterson outclass Joe Curran at Hampden Park. This time Benny asked for the price of a pair of boots, and certainly his own, tattered so much that they were kept together only by the string serving as laces, badly needed replacing.

I gave him a note myself, knowing full well to what purpose it would be used, but not having the iron in me to refuse. I watched him scuttle so hastily across the road to the public house, that he was almost run over in his anxiety to satisfy again the devil which had already taken him so far down the trail that has only one end.

When we got to Hampden that night there was Benny, like a barrel, begging for admission. He worked his way in, somehow. All alone, I did not see him speak to anyone in the course of the evening. Perhaps he was dreaming of the days when, in my opinion, he could have beaten both Paterson and Curran in the same night.

Almost certainly his dream world was more agreeable than the everyday one, in which he had no position other than that of the drunkard ex-fighter, always on the outside looking in. It was the last time I saw him alive. At the time I never guessed that he had only four weeks to live.

With the last week of July came the Glasgow Fair Week, and to the city came Jim Patterson's booth.

Benny saw a chance to earn a few bob, and tried to get himself a temporary job. Now, there was no more ardent supporter of Lynch in all Scotland than Big Jim. His feelings were displayed so that all might see, for over the entrance to the booth was a painting with the caption : 'Benny Lynch, when Flyweight Champion of the World.'

Yet here was that warrior on his uppers. Jim Patterson could see at a glance that Benny would never box again in his, or any other ring, for by this time it was apparent that Lynch was a desperately sick man. Giving him a little cash advance, the kindly booth proprietor told Benny to go home and come back when he felt better. And that was the last Patterson saw of his one-time idol.

Still hugging that dreadful secret to himself, Lynch continued to treat whisky as a food until his body could resist no more. The lonely struggle ended when at eight o'clock on the night of August 7th, he half walked, half crawled into the Southern General Hospital. At five o'clock next morning Benny breathed his last. The big fight was over.

It's funny how death brings people to their senses. Those who had cheered him in his triumphs and later jeered the ruin that had been Lynch gave him a fine send-off on his last journey when they laid him to rest in St. Kentigern's Cemetery at Lambhill, Glasgow. Benny would have been happy, for everyone in the sporting world was represented, from the highest to the lowest.

Millionaires were there. So were beggars. There were gentlemen and there were villains. Young and old,

115

male and female, the bigwigs of sport and the ordinary man-in-the-street. But whatever and whoever they were, most of them could not refrain from shedding a tear. A champion and a booth boxer openly wept.

Benny's 'ain' were there too. All of them. From Tom McCue and Sammy Wilson right up to Moss Deyong and John Macadam. Och aye, this was a grand farewell!

It was reminiscent of the fighter's biggest moments as the cortége slowly wound its way through the densely packed crowds which had come to pay their last respects to the little Scot who had inscribed his name indelibly in the annals of boxing history. Perhaps some mentally sought his forgiveness for having treated him shabbily, who knows?

At that moment the comparative trivialities which during his lifetime had seemed so important were forgiven and forgotten. Now his magnificent achievements were viewed in their true perspective, and one thing stood out clearly—he had been a superb champion. Whatever he may have been outside the ring, with his feet on the canvas he behaved like the aristocrat of boxing he was during the time he was at the top.

That was the reckoning. Benny had survived everything to take his place among the immortals of the roped square.

Ah well. Marking the spot where he lies stands the monument erected by his admirers, a marble headstone bearing the epitaph: 'To the memory of Benny Lynch, undefeated Flyweight Champion of the World. The first Scotsman ever to win a World Boxing Title.

Born 2nd April 1913. Died 8th August 1946. Erected by Boxing Fans. Always a Fighter.'

Another marble stone in the shape of an open book reads simply : 'From a few Gourock fans.'

From far and near came tokens offering testimony to the admiration of sports lovers the world over. A fit Lynch in the ring was invincible anywhere near his weight; but outside the ring John Barleycorn could always lick him. That was the tragedy.

But in passing Benny left a legacy for those who follow in his footsteps, for his grim struggle from booth fighter to world champion sets a shining example of grit and determination which should be the pattern for any boy aspiring to fame in the fight-game. While the other side of the story should serve as a warning to those who have already attained the heights.

Scotland lost the goods when Benny Lynch passed on from battling to bottling. A very sad affair indeed. May his soul rest in peace.

Part Two

HE CAME FROM BELOW

CHAPTER TWELVE

TEARS WERE OUT. FISH SUPPERS WERE IN.

THERE are many who hold that a humble beginning in life is a good thing, reasoning that from such a start progress can only be made upwards. If this be so, then the subject of my story started life in the right place, for he first saw the light of day—or as much of it as could be seen—from a one-apartment home in a tenement building at number 17, Florence Street, on the south-side of Glasgow.

Fortunately the only other occupants of the Lynch menage were father, mother and a brother, so that the one available bed stood up to the additional burden of the under-sized Benny.

Now Glasgow as a city, like the curate's egg, is good in parts. True, she has many gems of architecture such as the Art Galleries, the Municipal Buildings, the Stock Exchange together with many vast department stores in the centre of the city. But, though they are today gradually being demolished and then rebuilt, in the days of which I write there were, tucked away in the back-streets, incongruous tenement buildings of no known period, but cunningly designed so that the tenants might not be troubled by the circulation of too much air, nor yet again be dazzled by the glare of the sun. The Gorbals.

Here, of necessity, the communal life was practised to the full. One such dwelling was the Florence Street home of the Lynch family.

Small wonder, then, that the future world's champion was a puny, pasty-faced specimen of humanity, or that he remained so throughout his childhood. Early on in life, Benny's elder brother gave up the struggle and died during a bout of pneumonia.

Just how much this affected Benny will never be known. He did not shed many tears, for in his circle tears in a man were a sign of weakness and resulted in loss of face. It was all right for girls, but when a fellow reached the age of seven or eight, well, it just wasn't done to cry.

Having been enrolled at St. John's School and having been a keen playground sparmate of one Tom McCue, his senior by three years, it was a natural step for Benny to enlist in the St. John's Boys' Guild, which boasted its own boxing club.

Run by Father Fletcher, a Roman Catholic priest who was not averse to taking off his coat and dog-collar and having a go himself, this little outfit produced many boys who were later to make their names in the roped arenas. Among them were Johnny McGrory, who was to win the British and Empire featherweight titles in 1936 and was a life-long friend of Benny; Paddy Docherty, who was to oppose Lynch on no fewer than five occasions; together with such as Frank Erne, Tommy Steele, Billy Innes, George Lalloway and a host of others.

In such company Benny served his fighting apprenticeship. He emerged as a useful performer who tipped the beam at somewhere around the five-stone mark.

The family fortunes picked up a trifle and the removers took the Lynches to more commodious premises at Cumberland Lane. This was almost on the doorstep of the famous L.M.S. Rovers Club in Eglinton Street so, changing his stable, Benny became a 'Rover' and it was here that he blossomed forth as a midget boxer.

With Jimmy Cameron, a lad of equal stature, Lynch was drilled in the art of leading, blocking, slipping and feinting. By now he was a hard, lean boy who, when in action, moved with the grace of a ballet-dancer. His timing was uncanny, his anticipation perfect, with the result that an exhibition provided by Cameron and himself was hard to beat for sheer grace of movement and scientific skill.

Schoolboy boxing in those days was not as popular as it is now, yet wherever these two little 'Rovers' appeared, they brought the house down.

So, even at this early stage of his life, Benny was accustomed to the roar of the crowd—and how he loved it! In his little red singlet, striped pants and with his hair slicked back with vaseline, he was a champion to himself every time he ducked through the ropes. With a broad grin and hands clasped aloft he would acknowledge the plaudits of the crowd. This was the life; he was really SOMEBODY!

But the picture dissolved and with it, so it seemed, Benny's personality. As he changed into his everyday attire of much-darned jersey, patched trousers and old gym pumps life again became squalid and dull.

When he outgrew the stage when he could be billed as a midget, the youngster from the Gorbals became restless and moved about from club to club. Here, though, he was just another junior boxer and not so very successful at that. Was he to sink back into the rut after having savoured the rewards of fame? Not if he knew it. Benny sensed that somewhere, outside this little self-contained world of his, there was a bigger and better life to be found. The only question was how to find it.

On leaving school, Benny felt himself freed of some of the shackles and determined to find himself a job. He did not have to look far for, passing the Coliseum Picture House where he had often sneaked in through the back door, he could hardly fail to notice that structural alterations were in progress. Immediately seeking out the foreman, Lynch found that the job was running behind schedule and he was straightaway hired and entrusted with the responsible task of 'bilin' the cans.' In other words, he was appointed tea-boy.

After a while Benny reviewed the position. Calculating his wages and prospects of promotion he figured that, while tea-making was an honourable enough occupation, it was certainly no short-cut to the success which the Glaswegian was set on attaining in quick time.

So the time had come when he must take the plunge towards the fulfilment of the dream which he had cherished for years. He would earn his living with his fists. Having made up his mind, Benny became at once the man of action and presented himself without further ado at Tommy Watson's booth in Greendyke

Street where he knew it was possible to pick up almost
a full week's wages in one night.

"Can ye gie' me a fight, mister?"

The genial booth proprietor eyed the apparition
before him up and down, and indeed he did not have
to look far in either direction. Benny waited with bated
breath and, seeing that the kid was dead serious, Watson
decided to humour him.

"What weight are ye, son?"

"I'm seven-stone-six, but I'll box at flyweight."

"There's no one that sma' to put ye in with, but ye
can catch the gloves for my featherweight's challenge
on Saturday night and ye'll come to no harm."

"Ye needn't bother, Mister, I'll lick him."

It was at this point that fate took a hand in the
affairs of Benny Lynch. Fate in the form of Samuel
Wilson, a mine of information on all aspects of boxing.
There used to be a saying among Glasgow fight-fans
to the effect that "If it's no' in the rule-book, see Sammy
Wilson and he'll explain it."

Born, by coincidence, in the same street as Benny,
Sammy's one love was boxing. Sparring-partner to former Scottish lightweight champion Jim Gilmour, and
himself victor of many exciting struggles, Wilson was
now self-appointed foster-father to all Glasgow kids who
wished to set foot on the first rung of the fistic ladder.
In his unpretentious club at 49, Clyde Place, he coaxed,
wheedled or bullied to bring out the best in the half-
dozen or so aspirants to fame and fortune.

To these lads the place was more of a home than
a club, for the usual procedure on returning from a
show was to make for the club for a sumptuous meal

prepared by Sammy's sister, Star. Main dish at these banquets was invariably fish and chips, hot from the 'fry' shop on the corner.

On many occasions it was with misty eyes that Star Wilson watched the kids give their fish suppers 'a tanning,' for to them without doubt it was the main event of the evening. For the use of his premises, equipment, tuition and matchmaking duties Sammy charged the boys a mere sixpence a week. Which meant, of course, that the meals were 'on the house.'

Little did Wilson think, as he made his way to Tommy Watson's booth that night, that a long-cherished dream was at last to become a reality. For Sammy had always averred that someday he would discover a great champion hailing from the south-side.

As he entered the booth he was surprised to find the crowd whistling 'Pop goes the Weasel' and, glancing up at the ring, Sammy saw the inspiration for the tune in the person of the diminutive Benny who was jumping up and down like a puppet on a string as he warmed up in his corner having duly accepted the proprietor's challenge to 'all-comers' on behalf of the show's featherweight.

But soon the entire audience were gaping as they saw Benny box rings round the experienced booth scrapper, and they applauded wildly as he demonstrated exactly how the complete boxer should perform. Afterwards they showered the ring with coppers, and when these 'nobbins' were collected Lynch's share came to more than the five shillings he had been promised for the bout.

Such a reception did he receive that he boxed twice

more that night, and when he had finished Sammy Wilson made his way back-stage; this being the other side of a tarpaulin which hung from ceiling to floor.

"Hello, Sammy, who are ye lookin' for?" queried Watson.

"That kid Lynch ye had on."

"What dae ye think o' him, Sammy?"

"I'm no kiddin'," said Sammy. "I think that he's guid and that I can make something o' him so I'm guinta tak' him along o' me."

Meanwhile the subject of this conversation, elated at the turn of events, felt it time to intervene.

"Ye mean you're guinny tak' me in hand, Mister Wilson?"

"Aye, and ye can cut out the mister—Sammy's ma name."

"Well, seems ye've got yoursel' a manager, son," grinned Watson.

As the pair left the booth and made their way over the bridge to the south-side, Sammy outlined the rules and regulations of his organisation for the benefit of his new charge.

"The first thing you've got to do is learn to obey orders. D'ye hear?"

"O.K. Sammy."

"Ye'll maybe find ma methods of training a wee bit different from what ye've been used to, but what I say goes. Are ye still keen?"

"Aye Sammy."

"Right then. Tell your Dad to come down and see me tomorrow night."

Benny wended his way home as proud as a pea-

127

cock. He felt as if he was walking on air, and the glimmer of a smile broke over his small, dour face.

Dad Lynch appeared at the club next evening.

"Hello, Sammy, ma wee Benny tells me ye're going ta tak' him in hand. What dae ye think o' him?"

For once in a while the usually smiling face of Sammy Wilson was dead serious as he replied in a voice trembling with sincerity: "Let Benny come along o' me for a couple of years and I'll make him a champion!"

CHAPTER THIRTEEN

THEY ALL CAME ALIKE, EXCEPT MR. A. JOB

MEMBERSHIP of the Polytechnic, as Sammy's Club was known, gave young Lynch a new slant on life. No longer did he have to hang around street-corners during the long winter evenings, for the premises were open every night of the week. You could even get a game of billiards if you had a penny for the slot which worked the table lights, and if you were skint, well, there was always a warm fire and a cup of tea.

Weekly dances were run, girls being provided by the local talent. Yet Benny was notoriously shy on these occasions, a circumstance which caused much ragging and good-natured joking from the boys. Although he laughed it off, he was acutely conscious that his threadbare clothes did not match up to the natty suitings of some of the more affluent fellow-members. The disparity only served to increase Benny's burning desire to be 'in the money' so that he could be 'one of the boys' rather than just with them.

Thus it was a very determined young man who tackled his new manager.

"Sammy, I want you to fix me a fight."

129

Wilson dismissed the idea, saying "Naw, naw son. Ye've plenty of time; ye're no ready yet."

Then Benny played his ace. "Sammy, I chucked ma job, and if ye'll no get me matched I'll have no wages to take home at the end of the week."

Now these were hard times, and nobody knew better than Wilson just what the loss of a wage-packet would mean to the Lynch household. Cornered, the manager went off to see Jim McOnie, promoter of bi-weekly shows at The Ring in Gallowgate. When he returned he brought with him the glad news—"Ye're on for McOnie on Saturday."

Benny was delighted. "How much do I get Sammy?"

"Eighteen bob," was the reply. "I tried for a pound, but the house seconds have to get a shillin' each."

For the youthful Glaswegian the financial crisis was averted, temporarily at least. Eighteen bob for one night's work in the early days of 1931 was not bad. Not bad at all! He began to conjure up visions of the future. If he could fight twice a week, maybe even three times . . .

It is, I think, significant that Benny didn't even trouble to ask who his opponent was to be on that first occasion; a singular lack of interest in the class and status of the opposition which was to persist throughout his career. They all came alike to Lynch, and this was not an affectation but just an inborn confidence in himself which was part of his fighting make-up.

So, at last, a truly great fighter had been launched. Yet his path to the top was to prove anything but smooth, and after a year or so of 'bill-openers' during which he met Johnny Boag, Young Cairns, Matt Easdale, Jim Devanney, Jim McKenzie, Charlie Abrew and a host of others, the existence of B. Lynch of Glasgow was still recognised by the newspapers in only the smallest of type and down among the 'Other Results.'

Persevering, however, Benny found himself elevated from the bottom spot of all on promoters' advertising posters, and he was now competing in a grade where the cash rewards were a little better, while the opposition was a great deal more formidable.

Though not setting the heather afire among these better boys, Lynch acquitted himself creditably enough. One of his setbacks was a points verdict dropped to Freddie Tennant of Dundee, but in a return bout Benny did well to hold Freddie to a draw. This was a pretty good result for Lynch, as Tennant was considered to be in the running for a tilt at the Scottish title. More especially because the majority of fans present felt that the Glasgow boxer had done enough to win.

Up to now Benny had relied solely on his boxing ability to earn him victories, but it now looked as though he was beginning to develop a punch for, round about this time, he halted Charlie Deacon in the third round, Scotty Deans in the fourth and George McLeod in the fifth.

By this time, too, he had renewed acquaintance with former school and clubmate Paddy Docherty. As the pair set out on their professional careers at practically the same time and were of equal poundage, it was inevitable that sooner or later their paths should cross.

Paddy, now domiciled at Bridgeton in the East End of Glasgow, had won the Western District amateur flyweight title and, since commercialising his fists, had greatly impressed. Docherty was said to be 'really going places,' while Benny was the South-side hope for the big-time. So that the pairing of these two at Jim Gilmour's 'Premierland' provided a fine 'Local Derby.'

The bout itself provided a real fistic treat, with Lynch's graceful movements and crisp punching on the one hand and Docherty's bobbing, weaving and hit-and-get-away tactics on the other. At the end of the scheduled eight rounds, though, it was Paddy's hand that the referee held aloft, to proclaim him winner on points.

Benny took defeat philosophically, remarking to Paddy that he'd "do him next time." To which Docherty cracked back: "Don't be sae silly, mon, ye've nae chance."

Still, the warning was accompanied by Paddy's infectious grin, which had the effect of cementing their interrupted friendship—a friendship that was to stand the test of time and much keen rivalry.

Presumably Benny was stacking away his cash at this time, for Sammy Wilson met him at Hogmanay at the end of 1931, gaily attired in a brand new rig-out. Self-consciously he stood fingering his rolled lapels.

"Verra nice, Benny," said Sammy. "Verra nice indeed, but it must have set you back a bit."

"Sure it did," replied Benny. "Fifty bob, but it was worth it. Specially made for me. Och aye, it was well worth it!"

That new suit did things to Lynch, for it was the

fulfilment of a long-cherished dream. Gone was the old inferiority complex, and now, instead, he was really one of the boys.

It was, I suppose, a natural reaction that from here on dress became a sort of fetish with Benny. Certainly no matter in what precarious state his finances stood he always presented a well-groomed appearance.

Armed with his 'new-look,' it was not long before he was caught up in the social whirl and, together with Paddy Docherty and Bert Nicol, another of Wilson's boys, Benny did the round of the Glasgow dance-halls.

But with dancing at a shilling a session and fights coming only at the rate of one per month in 1932, the situation became grim. So grim, in fact, that Benny decided to go to work again. Even so, after a few weeks of employment as a rivet-heater in the shipyards, he came to the conclusion that things couldn't possibly be that bad.

Having gone through nine contests undefeated that year, Benny was paired with Paddy Docherty in a return. Despite their friendship, a bout between these two never once failed to evoke the 'needle' element, chiefly on account of the partisanship of their respective supporters. For the South Side and Bridgeton were keen rivals for supremacy in all sporting matters, and territorial pride was manifested on such occasions.

Lynch did not quite fulfil his promise to 'do' Paddy that November night, for after ten rounds he shared the honours of a drawn decision.

Following this, he was booked to top the bill at Watson's booth, but owing to some injury his advertised opponent was forced to cry off. Watson, however, knew where he could obtain a worthy substitute and at once sent off a telegram to one Andy Smith.

The latter deserves special mention, for he was one of those interesting characters who crop up from time to time in the annals of the boxing business. A native of Johnstone, a small township eleven miles outside Glasgow, Andy was the owner of a prosperous fruit business which incorporated a motor-lorry and a horse and cart. For his own pleasure, Smith ran a private car in addition. And this was the fellow who Watson was asking to deputise against Lynch.

Now men who ply their wares in a boxing booth normally do so purely for financial gain. Andy Smith was the exception, for though he didn't need any cash he just loved to fight.

Twenty-nine-year-old Andy had been doing this sort of thing for years. Not just in booths, either, for he had taken on Jim Higgins, Packy Cassidy and many other champions and near-champions.

Even now, at an age when he should have been content to look and act like a successful businessman, Mr. Smith couldn't resist the call to action. On receiving the wire Andy at once contacted his wife who, being used to such escapades, shrugged her shoulders, donned her white coat and took the wheel of the lorry while her husband high-tailed it to the big city.

Result of the affray was a points win for Lynch. Smith, who, though he had never scaled the heights in the ring, had the experience which enabled him to recognise a good 'un when he met one, realised that Benny had what it takes. Andy took an immediate liking to his young adversary, and suggested that Lynch should spend a short holiday with his wife and himself at Johnstone.

It was the first time that our little fighter had spent any length of time away from the smoky city, and the fresh air, combined with regular meals and plenty of fresh fruit, began to have effect; the pallid complexion of the town lad being replaced by a healthy tan.

Nor was training neglected. Smith saw to that, for among his many activities Andy ran the Caledonian Amateur Athletic Club. There Benny got plenty of sparring in the evenings, while two mornings a week were devoted to roadwork. What should have been a short visit lengthened into weeks, and in such surroundings he was fast approaching the peak of physical fitness.

Then Andy became restless as he contemplated his own holiday. Now, as far as vacations were concerned, Mr. Smith had a one-track mind. Not for him the delights of foreign travel and plush hotels. No, indeed. Where, he averred, could one find more holiday atmosphere and the spirit of carnival than in the fairground?

This pet theory was expounded to Benny, and Mrs. Smith again shrugged her shoulders. She knew what was coming but, being a wise woman, she also knew that there was nothing she could do about it.

Bubbling over with excitement and enthusiasm, Benny listened to his host's plan, which was that they should make a grand tour of the north of England, via the boxing booths, thus combining business with pleasure. When the limousine began its run out of Johnstone, Mrs. Smith was thoughtful as she waved goodbye to the two prospective booth boxers who were setting out for England and adventure.

CHAPTER FOURTEEN

FAIRGROUND FIGHTER

THE pair headed south and, some time after crossing the border into England, they broke their safari at Sunderland to join Len Johnson's booth. This marked a new phase in the life of the kid from the Gorbals, and though the fact that he would now be called on to tackle all-comers held no terrors for cocky Benny, in fact he had much to learn in this branch of his craft.

But he was not thrown in with the lions unprepared, for Johnson, fabulous old-time coloured middleweight from Manchester and a past-master in all the arts and crafts of ring warfare, took great pains to explain and list the pitfalls which lay in the path of the unwary booth-fighter.

Lynch, quite naturally, found himself at a disadvantage to begin with, since any opponent was necessarily an unknown quantity. Challengers at the booth fell into several categories, each requiring a different method of treatment. First there were the drunks, who arrived in various degrees of intoxication. Fortified by the spirit of Bacchus, they usually proclaimed their ability to lick anyone of around their own poundage.

They were far from being a nuisance; but instead

137

were a decided asset to the showman as they invariably put the audience in a good humour. Seldom, however, was a drunk accommodated unless he had a local reputation as a fighting man—and only then if the crowd insisted.

In such cases, the method adopted by the booth boys was not to dispose of the challenger quickly, but rather to 'gee with him,' in other words to carry him along and make him look as good as possible without his supporters realising that their man was the only one really trying.

Successfully administered, this treatment would result in the challenger returning the following day, convinced that being now sober he could anihilate the booth fighter with ease! The same remedy would again be applied, the staff boxer rationing his skill, punch and strength to suit that of his challenger. The process could be continued indefinitely, and was one that made for good business.

There were also the genuine aspirants to fistic fame, equipped with a supreme confidence in their own ability but little else. This type could prove dangerous at times, mostly on account of their total ignorance of the rules of boxing. Against them one came up against blows unmentioned in any instructional book as the earnest challenger came charging in, head down and arms swinging in all directions.

Most testing were the challenges of boys who had been, or still were, in the business themselves and saw a chance to earn a few shillings at the expense of the showman. These usually made a practice of challenging a lad somewhat lighter than themselves. As the show-man was not in a position to quibble too much about weight differences, booth fighters were often called on to concede poundage to challengers, and this could range from a couple of pounds to as much as a couple of stones.

Still, Benny took to the life and the routine like a duck to water, and was always thrilled as he stood with his colleagues on the platform in front of the marquee, while the 'barker' proclaimed their merits loud and long to the crowd.

That Lynch and Andy Smith provoked more comment than their fellows was not due to their physical proportions so much as to the fact that they were 'foreigners.' This was at once apparent from the tartan tammies perched jauntily on their heads.

It is a trait of Scotsmen that, when they travel, they like it to be known that they hail from the Land o'Burns and, being used to the road, Andy had at the outset of their journey placed the tammy on Benny's head with the strict injunction that it should stay put their return.

Yet little did the fruiterer guess that at a later date he was to place that same tammy on his companion's head on a much more auspicious occasion.

Came the challengers, and at first Andy with his wider experience tried to protect the fledgling by taking on the heavier and more formidable looking of the opposition in their class. None the less, before long, Benny was engaging all-comers and disposing of them in a manner that brought a smile of contentment to the face of the old maestro himself, Len Johnson.

Now and again there comes a time when challengers are scarce, and it is then that it becomes necessary for booth showmen to perpetrate a little harmless deception. It usually takes the form of some members of the entourage mingling with the crowd and assuming the role of challengers, or, as they term it in the trade, 'catching the gloves.'

Accepted procedure is that, when a volunteer offers to step into the ring, the booth owner tosses him a pair of gloves which he catches and thus accepts the challenge issued by the showman on behalf of one of his men.

When it was common knowledge in any particular district that there were no local aspirants among the smaller men, it was arranged that Andy Smith should catch the gloves for Benny, the result being a 'gee' fight. Now such a set-to is by no means a swindle, since the audience get full value for their money, seeing clever boxing coupled with crowd-pleasing tactics, which sometimes provide better entertainment than a 'straight' match.

Both Andy and Benny were keen to give of their best, with the result that tempers became frayed and the contest which was supposed to be a 'gee' developed into a 'needle' or grudge fight. It proved the hit of the evening and had the crowd yelling for more.

Len Johnson was not slow to spot Benny's potentialities, and that is not surprising because the former had in his heyday been one of the wiliest performers in the whole wide world. His experience told him that the Lynch kid was in a class above the rest. So enthusiastic was the coloured warrior that he penned a letter extolling the Glaswegian's virtues to sportswriter Elky Clark, former British, Empire and European flyweight champion who had himself come within an ace of bringing home the World's title after an epic battle with Fidel La Barba at Madison Square Garden in New York. Elky, who also hailed from Glasgow, was favourably impressed and promised to watch the progress of his fellow-townsman.

Meanwhile that caged-in feeling had hit Andy Smith again. The open road called, and despite the entreaties of the downcast Len Johnson, the Smith bandwagon moved on again.

At West Hartlepool the boys met Battling Sullivan and his booth. 'The Bat,' as he was affectionately tagged, was the father of Johnny Sullivan, later to reign briefly as British and Empire middleweight champion, but Johnny was only in his childhood at the time of which I write. Andy decided that these surroundings were the very thing he and his pal needed, so Sullivan found himself the possessor of two new flyweights.

Once, when challengers were few and far between, Benny took a leaf out of Andy's book by offering to go out into the crowd and catch the gloves for his pal. But Sullivan wouldn't hear of it.

"You know I make our challengers speak up and state their experience," he said. "Why, man, as soon as you opened your mouth they'd know you are both Scots and suspect a fixed fight. Then there'd be a riot!"

Suddenly Benny had a brainwave. He didn't need to open his mouth; he could act dumb and make out he was a mute!

141

Taking his place among the audience, therefore, he contrived, by much waving of his hands and making strange sounds, to convey the impression that he wished to take on dwarfish Andy.

That night Lynch is said to have put up a performance which would have done credit to an Irving or an Olivier. So intent on his act was he that he failed to take note of the bell which signalled the end of the bout, and had to be forcibly directed to his corner. But he had captured the imagination of the crowd, and when the battle was declared a draw both boys were given a great ovation and coins were showered into the ring before the spectators dispersed.

One man, though, felt that Benny and he had something in common, and therefore came round to congratulate him in sign language—for he was a deaf-mute!

Luckily this man, despite his misfortune, was blessed with an outsize sense of humour. On having the truth scribbled down on paper so that he might understand, he saw the funny side of it, and made it clear that he would keep mum in more ways than one.

It was with genuine regret that Andy and Benny bade farewell to the Sullivans — particularly to Ma Sullivan, a kindly lady who had looked after them both and who had done her utmost to be a real mother to Benny. He meant to keep his promise to return soon, and little did he realise that this was goodbye to the booths, if not for good, then at least for some considerable time.

With the arrival of the two rovers back at Andy's home in Johnstone came one of those queer twists of fate which govern the affairs of men. Smith had the misfortune to fracture an ankle at work, which meant that Benny had no alternative other than to return to Glasgow. This brought to an end his lengthy holiday, and with it his close association with Andy Smith. For Johnstone never saw him again.

Back home in Glasgow, the Gorbals warrior eagerly related his doings to Sammy Wilson, and with the impatience of youth demanded that his manager should fix him to meet Scottish flyweight champion Jim Campbell.

Imperturbable Sammy refused to be rushed. "Ye'll get a fight wi' Campbell aw right, I can promise ye that. But only when I'm sure ye have the beating o' him, and not before." Nevertheless, Sammy got busy fixing other outings for his charge, and Benny's first bout on his return from the booths was over ten rounds with Joe Aitken of Manchester, an affair which the Scot won easily on points.

For some time after this Lynch seemed to be making little headway, and impatiently he chafed at the bit in his anxiety to achieve big things, while Wilson continually reminded him that there were quite a number of obstacles to be cleared from his path before he could reasonably expect recognition as a contender for his native title.

Chief of these hurdles was his old rival Paddy Docherty, who was reckoned to be on a par with Lynch at this period.

"Then let's get on wi' it," said Benny. "Ye fix the fights and I'll clear the obstacles out o' ma path."

This particular obstacle was not so easily cleared, for at their next meeting a draw was the outcome after ten hard-fought stanzas. Benny felt frustrated, but Sammy was still calmly confident, and when three weeks later the pair met yet again Benny finished a clear winner. Now he felt that he could get somewhere.

Certainly things were looking up, for this and other victories were bringing him favourable newspaper mentions, and he was almost certain to be included in the eliminators to find a challenger for Jim Campbell. Just when he was meeting better-class boys and the wind seemed set fair, up popped bogey-man Docherty once more.

Their final meeting resulted in another draw, yet it marked the real beginnings of Lynch's rise to fame, for from here on he never looked back.

Among his opponents around this time was another Bridgeton boy named Alec Farries. A tough and crafty performer, Farries had tangled with some of the best in the game though Benny seems to have had the Indian Sign on him. For on each of their four meetings Alec finished the loser. The last of these is notable, because it was then that Lynch 'discovered' what was to become his famous left hook.

The fourth session saw him spot an opening and toss this blow to his rival's body. To the general surprise Farries went to the boards and, although he beat the count, the referee saw that Alec was badly damaged and stopped the fight. And Farries had never previously been stopped throughout his long career.

Benny must surely have thought to himself: "That was some punch if it was good enough to put paid to a guy like Farries. I must concentrate on it and try to perfect it." Thus was faith in his left hook born, but

144

what Lynch never suspected was that, on the day of the contest, Alec had sweated off several pounds and gone without any fluid in order to come in at the stipulated weight of eight stone two, and had entered the ring weak as a kitten. Actually, he spent a week in bed after the battle recuperating, not from Lynch's 'dig,' but from the effects of the stewing and dehydrating process.

CHAPTER FIFTEEN

SAMMY WILSON AT THE HELM

IN every good fighter's career there comes the time when he emerges from 'small fry' competition to tackle the champions and near-champions. The time comes, too, when he emerges from small-hall bills and faces suddenly the huge crowds who attend the major promotions. That first reaction to the big occasion can make or break a fighter.

The early summer of 1933 marked the transitional period for Benny, and here one can detect the shrewd handling of Sammy Wilson who was obviously picking each opponent with a view to consolidating his protegé's position as a contender for the Scottish title. Now Sammy was coming out into the open with the news that his fighter was ready to step into the big-time, and he was desirous of driving this fact home to the world in general and to the British Boxing Board of Control in particular.

For his debut among the big-shots, Lynch was paired with former Scottish flyweight kingpin Jim Maharg, who had relinquished the title won by Campbell. It was by far Benny's toughest assignment to date, for Maharg was a clever boxer who also packed a hefty wallop. He had narrowly missed becoming British champion the previous autumn when being disqualified against Jackie Brown of Manchester.

It is typical of the see-saw of fame in the fight-game that, just a few months before their clash in May '33, Benny had felt privileged to act as sparring-partner to Maharg, and the fact that he had received three pounds a week had not detracted from the honour.

The ex-champ had forfeited the Scottish crown because he could not come in at the required eight stone. It was an open secret that he had his work cut out to scale the stipulated eight-two for the 12-rounder with Lynch. Thus it was Benny who made the running, while Maharg was quite content to box on the defensive.

Perhaps afraid that he might not be able to stay the journey through having impaired his stamina by weight-making, Maharg persevered with his evasive action until the half-way mark, gradually increasing his pace until the last two sessions, when he really turned on the heat. But the effort came too late and referee the late George Dingley—this was his first glimpse of Benny—had no hesitation in naming Lynch the winner.

With this fine scalp dangling from his boxer's belt—or should it be kilt?—Wilson proceeded with the build-up and three weeks later Benny was lined-up with the Irish eight-stone champion, Billy Warnock, who was battered into submission inside eleven rounds. Though, as we have already seen, the Irishman was to be fully avenged at a later date by his brother, Jimmy.

A fortnight went by, then Kid Hughes, the Welsh titleholder, was also accounted for, the towel being skied from his corner in the ninth round.

Lynch was on the way up now, but he still had

a long way to travel. True, he was getting plenty of publicity and his followers were steadily increasing, but that much desired meeting with Jim Campbell was not yet in sight.

Nevertheless, life was pretty good. The money was coming in a little faster, not enough to throw around, mind, but he did own three or four suits, and with the confidence that cash brings, Benny was becoming a good mixer in his own sphere. There were afternoons at the cinema, dancing in the evenings and, best of all, the ladies. Of course, he had had several girl friends in the past, but now there was one who was different. D'ye ken?

Actually our Benjamin had first made her acquaintance quite a while ago. He used to tell his old schoolmate, Tom McCue, about her—chiefly because he knew Tom was a good listener and wouldn't laugh at him. For Benny was dead serious, and though he was getting used to the limelight and revelled in it, he liked to come off the merry-go-round once in a while and attempt to sort things out in their true perspective. Aye, deep down Benny had a desire for the security of a good home, a wife and children.

Snag was that the lady wasn't too keen, for after all boxing was a precarious sort of business. Now, if her man had a steady job, with prospects of making some money . . . . but the idea of Benny in a steady job was altogether too far-fetched.

Nevertheless, he did settle down to the task he already had in hand. Late nights were cut right out, and every morning he was out at six o'clock burning up the roads around Cathkin Braes. The vision of a fight with Campbell had become just about the most important thing in the world.

With plenty of sparring at the Polytechnic and other clubs around the Gorbals which he visited, Benny was in peak condition when a series of eliminating bouts were announced and he never had any doubts concerning his ability to fight his way through them.

There were plenty of others with similar ideas, for when applications for inclusion were invited no fewer than twenty-one names were forwarded. But, money being scarce, only seven of the applicants kicked in with the required one pound deposit, leaving Scotty Adair, Tony Ryan, Jackie Ryan, Jim Brady, Willie Vogan, Boy McIntosh and, of course, Benny Lynch to form the pack that was hot on the heels of Jim Campbell.

Lynch was first paired with Vogan whom he disposed of in the second round with a lovely right hook to the chin. It looked as though he would have his work cut out in the next stage, however, for he was drawn against Blantyre's Boy McIntosh, a fighter with a big reputation as a KO king following a long string of inside-the-distance wins.

Now, there was a match that would have attracted a capacity crowd anywhere, quite apart from the fact that there was a South-side versus East-end element about it. For although McIntosh hailed from Blantyre, he fought in the colours of the Dalmarnock Club in Bridgeton, run by the late George Aitchison who was reckoned by many to be the most knowledgeable trainer-manager in the game.

For more than forty years George had been turning out champions galore, and any boy who had Aitchison in his corner had the benefit of that great wealth of experience.

Even so, the wisdom of Solomon himself would have availed McIntosh little that night, because Benny was a smooth-running fighting machine. Almost before the clang of the opening bell had died away, he was across the ring and wading two-fisted into his man to take the bewildered McIntosh right out of his stride.

This process continued in the second, and the famed Lynch left hook to the short ribs and stomach was much in evidence. The Boy was given absolutely no chance to land one of his 'McIntosh Specials,' and by the end of the third it had become a one-horse race. McIntosh was being subjected to a real shellacking, but no one could dispute his gameness for he kept coming back for more.

The end came in the fourth, when Benny, fighting like a demon, punched his man to a standstill and McIntosh dropped to the boards completely exhausted to be counted out.

It was a fine victory, and it did Lynch a power of good in his hometown, for now even the East-enders began to admit that he might be a worthy opponent for Campbell at that. To Benny it had been a mere workout, and a week later he travelled southwards to West Bromwich to add another fine scalp to his growing list by decisively outpointing midlander Bert Kirby, a former British flyweight champion.

Two weeks more and, at Liverpool Stadium, the Scot was held to a draw over ten rounds by Bob Fielding of Wrexham. This brought to a close a year in which he had risen from the small-time to something approaching fame. For Benny was now making the headlines, and people who had never met him were nodding to him in the street.

Life was just a bowl of cherries; at twenty the world was at his feet. He had never felt better in his life. Much bigger plaudits were still to come, for the Gods were smiling on him.

At the beginning of 1934 Benny enhanced his reputation still further and advanced a step nearer his objective by qualifying to meet Jim Campbell. He defeated Jim Brady on points over twelve rounds in a stern but uninspiring final eliminator at Edinburgh, and just seven days later followed up by knocking out Salford's Freddy Webb with a left hook to the body in the third round.

And now came a highlight; Benny's first appearance on a big championship bill. At the Kelvin Hall in Glasgow his fellow-townsman, Johnny McMillian, was due to meet Seaman Tommy Watson for the latter's British featherweight championship, and in the chief supporting contest Lynch was matched with his initial Continental opponent in Carlo Cavagnoli of Italy. Carlo came with the reputation of being one of the best flyweights in Europe.

Though he feigned disinterest, the wee Scot must have been impressed by the pomp and ceremony preceding the fight, for Cavagnoli attracted as much interest as the championship contestants. He and Nick Cavalli, his manager, were greeted at the station by a large number of Italians who were locals.

Lynch remained in the background, but he got his publicity the day after the fight, when the headlines

151

screamed enthusiastically of what they announced to have been the finest performance of his career. Yes, Benny rose to the occasion in style.

It was indeed an impressive scene that the solemn-faced kid from the backstreets gazed on as his gloves were adjusted in the corner. All round him was a huge sea of faces, and Benny goggled with amazement at the boiled shirts and evening gowns of the ringsiders. As his eyes wandered further back over the 11,000 odd who packed the great hall, the dress of the customers became more informal.

He looked ill-at-ease as he glanced around, searching for his 'ain folk' with their cloth caps and mufflers. If they were too far back to be seen from under the glaring ring arclights, their hero must have been re-assured by the war-cry which came from the bleachers:

"Come on, Benny lad!"

Sure enough, Benny answered the call as Cavagnoli, short and stocky, advanced in a crouch, lithe and ready to spring in like a tiger. He did spring, only to be met by a ramrod straight left that stopped him in his tracks. Again he led, and again was brought up short.

The Italian looked distinctly puzzled, for when he tried to slip that straight left, Lynch switched to left hooks which were equally accurate yet a good deal more powerful and damaging.

Changing his tactics in the second round, Lynch gave a polished display of footwork, sidestepping the rushes of his aggressive adversary and clipping him as he floundered by with snappy hooks. The third saw Benny's left hook to the body in operation, but Carlo was tough and he could take it. He could dish it out, too, if only he could get in close.

In the fifth session, those hooks to the midriff had Cavagnoli gasping and hanging on, but not for nothing was he rated so highly: he came back full of fight, to swing a right for the jaw which must have finished the fight had it landed. But Lynch moved his head in classic style to allow it to fly harmlessly past.

From this point on, Carlo was reduced to being little more than a punch-bag for Benny. What a punch-bag, though, for this one kept bouncing back like a rubber-ball on a string till the crowd began to wonder what was holding Carlo up. At the final bell, Cavagnoli was still upright.

Though he hadn't won a single round of the ten he had never ceased trying and the Scots, who love a good loser, gave him an ovation that must have made him feel that his efforts had been worth while.

As to Benny, well, the fans went berserk. The sustained 'Hampden Roar' of the packed house was taken up by hundreds of people swarming in the street outside the fight-hall. Lynch had won fame overnight; he was a hero and an idol.

CHAPTER SIXTEEN

AN AMBITION ACHIEVED

B ENNY returned to the more homely setting of the Adelphi Stadium in Florence Street for his next bout, in which Londoner George Low was forced to retire in the second round having been on the receiving end of some of the Scot's deadly left hooking. And that was Lynch's last outing before he settled down to the more serious business of preparing for the long-awaited crack at Jim Campbell, involving as it would his native flyweight title.

Campbell never under-estimated an opponent, and he went into special training at Wick in the extreme north of Scotland. Lynch, on the other hand, continued to do his roadwork around Cathkin Braes and his sparring at the Polytechnic.

When the morning of 16th May dawned, the Lynch camp were calmly confident, as well they might be, for their challenger had youth on his side, and by virtue of his recent displays was more than a little favoured by the critics. While Campbell, though strong and still apparently as fast as ever, was considered to be approaching the veteran stage. But Jimmy had a vast following who were convinced that he would still be the champion when it was all over.

The promoter was the same George Dingley who had refereed some of Benny's earlier bouts, and he had chosen for his venue the Olympic Stadium or, as it was more commonly known, the Nelson Grounds. This was actually a greyhound stadium which adjoined Parkhead, the ground of the Glasgow Celtic Football Club.

Bearing in mind current prices for big-fight nights and, indeed, even those for the small-hall tournaments, it is worth recording that for this fistic feast charges ranged from one shilling to eight bob. Additionally, in contrast to today, Glasgow fight-fans then had three or four shows a week to choose from, most of them with ringside prices in the region of three-and-sixpence. So, if they forked out as much as eight shillings, they expected something extra special!

And this time they certainly got it, for the contest proved to be a ding-dong struggle from first to last and was fought on the expected lines, with Campbell the fighter rushing in to get to close quarters and Lynch the boxer depending on outfighting to carry him through to victory.

The champion began true to form. Crouching low, he stalked his man, waiting and watching while Benny tried to pierce his oyster-like defence with a few tentative left leads. Then, like a flash, Campbell was in and rapping three sharp uppercuts to Lynch's chin before transferring his attention to the midsection and bundling his man on to the ropes. The Gorbals boxer managed to sidestep clear, but Jim came forward again to score with solid body punches and take the first round.

Campbell kept up his terrier-like tactics in the second, but they only served to rouse Lynch who joined in with a two-fisted body attack which forced the champion back across the ring and into a neutral corner.

Both men were warming to their work now, and the third saw Benny trying to measure his man up with a long left hand before bringing his right into play. But every time he did this, Campbell manoeuvred to slip inside and beat a fast tattoo on his ribs.

The fourth brought a toe-to-toe slam in mid-ring during which Campbell was nailed with a hard right. Again, right on the bell, the champion was clearly shaken by a terrific left hook.

In the fifth Campbell was warned to keep his punches up and Lynch, who was adjudged guilty of holding and hitting, was also reprimanded. Halting the battle to lecture both boxers, referee Gus Hart made it abundantly clear that he would stand no nonsense. His rebuke had the desired effect, for both boys resumed at a pace that had the crowd wild with excitement.

There was little or nothing to choose between them at the half-way mark; but then, emerging from a clinch in the ninth with his right eye cut, the champion gesticulated that Lynch was illegally using his head. This obviously annoyed Benny, and he tore after his rival in a way that brought the crowd to their feet as Campbell back-pedalled frantically.

So it went on at a murderous pace, with the veteran titleholder showing no sign of fatigue. Instead, he came back to dictate his own pace as he finessed for position, sometimes slipping punches, sometimes blocking them, but always with the one object of getting in close.

When the bell brought them to the centre of the ring for the final stanza it was still anybody's fight.

Lynch now made the running, hitting out with both hands to the face and body. Jim countered strongly but a left hook to the solar plexus brought him up short for a moment. Yet still the champ moved forward, and the bout ended as it had begun — with Lynch the boxer engaged in repelling the attacks of Campbell the slugger.

Came the bell and an expectant hush fell over the crowd. It had been that kind of fight — nobody knew for certain who had won.

As he watched the referee lift Benny's glove in token of victory, Jim Campbell's face was a study. It bore a look of utter amazement, which was replaced a few moments later by one of infinite sadness, then finally by a smile as the gallant ex-champion sportingly crossed the ring to congratulate Benny while the Master of Ceremonies announced it to the crowd: "The winner and new flyweight champion of Scotland—Benny Lynch."

Aye, Benny had won, but not very convincingly. Many people in the crowd were displeased with the verdict, and they expressed their feelings with a storm of booing. Campbell, too, was far from being satisfied, nor, for that matter, was Lynch.

This was not the triumph he had dreamed of during the long months of waiting. Sure, he wanted the title more than anything else in the world, but with it he desired the unanimous applause of the crowd that greets a worthy champion.

When he mentioned his doubts and fears to Sammy Wilson, that worthy maintained that Benny had finished a clear winner even though he quite understood how the kid felt about it all.

"Wha' dae ye want to do, son—fight him again?"

"Aye, Sammy, it's the only thing to do," replied the newly-crowned champion.

The practice of holding on to titles jealously without defending them overmuch is a habit with some champions, but this was not so with Benny Lynch. The six months' grace allowed after a title fight? Oh no! Six weeks was too much, but this was the soonest that the return could be arranged. Campbell, naturally, jumped at the chance and the second meeting was fixed to take place at Cathkin Park, itself the home pitch of Scottish soccer's Third Lanark club.

Time passes slowly when one is young, especially if the youngster is particularly looking forward to some future event. It is only when one gets older that the days, weeks and years flit by. Six weeks was one hell of a long time to Benny; far too long to remain inactive.

Thus a mere two weeks after winning his crown found him matched with Evan Evans of Wales, whom he punched to a standstill inside three rounds, the referee terminating the proceedings with the Welshman draped helpless across the ropes.

Just forty-eight hours later at Parkhead Arena Peter Miller, a 'Geordie,' succumbed in the eighth session leaving Benny with some four weeks in which to attune himself for the defence of his laurels.

That night in late June found the turnstiles at Cathkin Park clicking merrily, as 16,000 fans poured in in expectancy of another exciting encounter.

The majority of the critics were non-committal. On

158

the face of it the affair was wide open, although Campbell, with his wider experience, was conceded a good chance of regaining his title.

Lynch's entourage, however, simply radiated confidence. To Benny this was no ordeal but a chance to redeem himself; a chance to prove that there had been no mistake the first time and that he was indeed the better man. And he did just that, leaving no room for doubt whatsoever. After the opening round he outboxed, outfought and outgeneralled Campbell to win decisively on points.

It was Benny's night, for he proved himself the complete copybook boxer and gave a classic display of all the arts and crafts which together make up the science of glove-fighting.

Vainly did Campbell try to get to close quarters, for Lynch's timing was perfect and his counter-punching provided a cast-iron barrier that the ex-champ was powerless to penetrate. On the few occasions when Jim did get close, Benny either deftly turned him into thee ropes and danced away or else side-stepped to send his adversary hurtling across the ring through the force of his own momentum.

By the end of the eighth Lynch was well out in front and was now beating Campbell at his own game. Varying straight leads with hooked attacks, the idol of the Gorbals tied his man up inside and then launched a volley of short-arm blows to the midsection.

Campbell presented a difficult target as he crouched bent practically double with forearm crossed across his chest and chin well down into his shoulder. Lynch, though, kept pounding away at his biceps, shoulders and anything else that stood in his way and he didn't pull his punches. As a result of this it was not too long before Jim's arms began to sag.

From the tenth round onwards the former champion took a terrible lacing but, game as they make 'em, he kept punching. It was more than Benny dared to do to let up for a single moment, for the dour and grimly determined Campbell was still full of fight and was always dangerous. Yet even the most short-sighted observer could scarcely have failed to spot the writing on the wall.

Only his indomitable spirit carried him through the last round, for Lynch went all-out for a knockout and sent his man crashing to the canvas half-way through the session with a left-right-left combination to the jaw. Valiant Campbell rose at 'four,' but only to meet an onslaught which sent him staggering across the ring. Yet he just refused to go down, and although Benny hit him with every blow in the book he was still tottering and reeling on rubbery legs when the bell proclaimed the end of the battle—and the fact that Jim was a well beaten ex-champion. For the crowd were roaring in exultation as they acclaimed their hero. Benny was back on his pedestal.

As he waved in acknowledgment of the cheers of his fans, Lynch must have experienced a thrill of satisfaction. At last his 'ain folk' accepted him as a worthy Scottish titleholder, which meant an ambition achieved.

But shrewd Sammy Wilson was looking much further ahead. For he realised that this was only the beginning for Benny, and he was already forming great plans for the future.

Meanwhile, as a bonus for capturing the Scottish championship, Sammy presented Benny with a gold pocket watch. The fighter, in his turn, gave Sammy a timepiece, but proposed that he should arrange for it to be inscribed as having come from the Scottish champion.

Wilson, however, thought this would be just a waste of time, as Benny was sure to go on to annex far bigger honours. "Why not," he suggested, "let the inscription simply read 'Flyweight Champion' so that the rest can be added at a later date?"

Benny fell in with the idea and, as we have seen, went on to win premier honours in his division. Yet somehow or other he never got around to having that gift fully engraved. And as long as he lives Sammy Wilson will carry around with him the watch that bears the inscription : "To my manager, Sammy Wilson, from Benny Lynch, Flyweight Champion." Just that and nothing more.

People questioning Sammy about the value of that timepiece have always received the same answer. Staunch Sammy would tell them wistfully: "Like the man that gave it to me, it's absolutely priceless."

CHAPTER SEVENTEEN

HE WHO FIGHTS AND RUNS AWAY . . . . !

W HEN manager Wilson announced that Lynch's next opponent would be Maurice Huguenin from France, many eyebrows were raised and there was quite an outcry in the press, the general view being that Sammy was pushing his protegé along a little too fast.

After all, the Frenchman could boast a victory over former world champion Young Perez, and he had in addition boxed a draw with the then reigning French kingpin, Valentin Angelmann, who was currently rated number one contender for world honours.

To a large percentage of Scottish fight-fans the match seemed sheer suicide. But Sammy Wilson recognised it as a golden opportunity; while to Benny it was just another fight. And what a fight it turned out to be, for Huguenin was a real tough guy who carried a sledge-hammer wallop in addition to possessing not inconsiderable skill as a boxer.

It was, in fact, this bout that proved once and for all to quite a few of those who really knew him that Benny had all the qualities which go to make a champion. Besides his undoubted natural talent, he showed in this set-to that he owned the right temperament for the big-time, plus the ability to take it as well as to dish it out.

Cathkin Park was the venue, pride of place on that 8th August bill going to Benny's former school and clubmate, Johnny McGrory, who became Scottish featherweight champion by laying low Jim Cowie of Dundee in the third round. This result ensured that Benny himself entered the ring in a happy frame of mind, for in the dressing-room he had shown far more concern over Johnny's fracas than his own.

With the knowledge that his pal had won, Lynch wended his way down the aisle to the ring with a broad, impudent grin lighting up his features as the capacity crowd rose and gave him a tumultuous welcome.

During the preliminaries he sat listening to the last-minute instructions from Sammy Wilson, looking as though he hadn't a care in the world. As he caught the eye of friends seated tensely at the ringside he comforted them with either a sly wink or a cheery nod before answering his mentor with his usual : "O.K., Sammy."

With the timekeeper's cry of "Seconds out, Time !" Benny had plenty to think about, for Huguenin was across the ring like a tornado, tossing punches from all angles. And they weren't slaps, either, so the Scot back-pedalled as fast as his legs would carry him round the ring while he cautiously weighed up the opposition.

Monsieur Maurice intended going places and he wanted to get there fast. Lynch was taken completely out of his stride and was given no chance to settle down, for when Huguenin sought a respite from hurling punches he just hung on to Benny and forced the latter to expend energy through throwing him off. The

163

Frenchman was strong and dangerous right enough, but Benny was more annoyed than hurt when he got back to his corner at the conclusion of the opening round.

"This guy can hit, Sammy," he muttered as he sat down.

"I know, son. Ye'll hae tae gradually wear him down, so keep plugging away at the heart."

Benny tried to obey orders, but Maurice behaved as if he had overheard them, for he gave the Scot no breathing space through his tactics of sticking close and holding on like grim death. Two or three times Lynch glanced at the referee when he was tied up in a clinch, but apparently that official could see nothing wrong, so the Gorbals warrior decided to take matters into his own hands.

He had not fought his way through the booths and most of the tough joints in Scotland without learning the tricks of the trade. Actually it is a safe assumption that he knew them all, but this was one of the few occasions when he resorted to a trick, and then it was done without malice but with the spirit of impishness which helped make Benny what he was.

With Huguenin hanging on like a leech, Lynch brought his free hand round the back and slapped his opponent on the shoulder. Now it is quite common practice among referees to do this when they wish to draw a boxer's attention to the fact that he is holding with one hand and must 'break away,' so, thinking that this was what was happening, the Frenchman stepped back quickly before he realised that the ref was actually well away and in front of him.

Surprised, he half turned to face the ref and so

allowed himself to be tagged with a whale of a left hook. Swinging round, he found Benny grinning like a Cheshire cat. Maurice nodded briefly, but his expression implied that he wouldn't be caught with that one a second time.

As the rounds went by the Scot eased into his stride, gradually got the hang of things and found that his body punching was most effective in stemming his opponent's rushes. By the fifth Benny had made up the leeway and it looked plain sailing when, suddenly, something happened.

To Benny it must have felt as though the roof had caved in. A pile-driving blow to the pit of the stomach knocked all the breath out of his body, and for a moment he was helpless. Involuntarily his arms sank down in sympathy, but biting hard on his gumshield he kept threatening with his left as if he was about to throw it.

The Frenchman had sampled that left hook before and he didn't relish it, so, rather than risk having to absorb another, he hung back and allowed Benny time to recover. Unless he chances to read this, presumably Maurice will never know just how near he came to clinching a victory over the great Benny Lynch!

From this point the Scot gradually gained the ascendancy by dint of clever boxing. Good left leading followed by some powerful right crosses slowed down the fiery Gaul sufficiently to enable Benny to secure a hard-earned decision.

After such a gruelling affray Lynch might have been excused had he chosen to indulge in a lengthy lay-off, but this fighter from fightville just could not tolerate inactivity and a further three weeks saw him squaring up in a return to Dundee's Jim Brady who had specially requested this chance to redeem himself.

Again it was an unspectacular affair, and although Lynch won on points he did not shine against Brady's spoiling tactics and thus disappointed the less knowledgeable of his supporters. Which was just too bad, for the very next day all the newspapers carried big headlines : "Lynch to fight most important battle of his career."

This was an understatement, for Benny had been pitted against the aforementioned Valentin Angelmann. Now Angelmann was right out of the top drawer, for already he had fought Jackie Brown three times for the world title and on the last occasion, some three months previously at Belle Vue, Manchester, Brown had been generally considered fortunate to retain his title when the referee rendered a drawn verdict.

For this vital contest Benny had almost four weeks to get into shape, and to the Scottish camp this was more than sufficient. The reader must realise that, at this period, Lynch's whole life was one continual round of training, interspersed with bouts at regular intervals. This ensured that he was always in fine fettle.

What was necessary was to decide on a plan of campaign. This was always an important feature of Benny's training, for Sammy Wilson ordered different tactics to suit—or rather, not to suit—the style of an opponent.

Those who dropped in at the Polytechnic to watch the Scot in training workouts left with the impression that he didn't look so good. Though he moved at top speed it was in the wrong direction, for he allowed the sparring-partners to chase him around the ring. It was the same right up to his final gym session, and most of the experts assessed him as being a good thing to take second place.

Impresario Dingley had enlisted the aid of practically everyone bar the weather-man in presenting this fistic extravaganza. For Wednesday, September 26th turned out to be a day of incessant rain, which cut down the attendance from an estimated 30,000 to somewhere in the region of 10,000.

Yet at least for an hour or so those who did brave the elements enjoyed the pulse-raising spectacle of a memorable struggle for supremacy between two perfectly-matched boys, among the best in the world at their weight.

The bout opened at a lively pace, Angelmann advancing across the ring to ram in a couple of lefts to the body while Lynch countered on the retreat with head punches. The Frenchman was boxing in top gear, and the Scot was forced backwards round the canvas.

As Lynch consistently backed away, those sessions at the Polytechnic began all at once to make sense. Each of those sparring-partners had played the role of Angelmann. Benny was fighting a planned campaign, and though it wasn't too apparent to those in the rear of the crowd he was doing nicely, stopping only to counter before retreating again and so deliberately drawing his man in.

The effect of this was noticeable near the end of the stanza, when Lynch suddenly halted and Valentin came in to receive a volley of lefts and rights to the head. But he was tough, was this continental, and wormed his way inside to batter Benny about the body.

Retreating again in the second, an Angelmann rush had the Glaswegian seemingly pinned on the ropes but, bouncing off, he got home with a vicious left to the ribs. Fancy footwork was thwarting the Frenchman's sustained aggression.

By the fourth Lynch was getting the measure of his man, and it was only occasionally that Angelmann's strength got him to close quarters. In the latter half of the session Lynch again stopped dead in his tracks, and the toe-to-toe exchanges which followed had the crowd cheering wildly. This time it was the Frenchman who was first to break off.

There was a great deal of holding in the ensuing round and Angelmann, after being spoken to by referee Jack Smith, became erratic and missed badly with wild swings while Benny scored freely to head and body alike.

Superb ringcraft plus an accurate straight left kept the exchanges open in the sixth, and the Scot's left glove was again the dominating factor in the seventh, Anglemann's successes in the clinches becoming few and far between.

The desperate Frenchman threw caution to the wind in the eighth. Benny, no longer able to resist the temptation, met him half-way and they exchanged blows non-stop in the centre of the ring for a full minute while the rain-sodden fans forgot all about their discomfort.

A new aspect of the battle was disclosed in the ninth when Lynch took over as aggressor. Three times he rocked his rival with combination blows to the jaw and landed almost at will with his leads. The fire had gone out of Angelmann.

With victory within his grasp, Lynch was now confidently ringing the changes between boxing and slugging, but always carrying the fight to his man who had to soak up a great deal of punishment.

Angelmann would not admit defeat, however, and the penultimate round saw him come again with renewed vigour. Finding his way close, he connected with a crushing right to the midsection and Lynch gave ground. Quick to seize the advantage, the visitor followed up throwing vicious head punches with either fist, but the local idol rode out the storm and his left hand kept Angelmann at bay until the bell.

The twelfth and final session was a complete reversal of the first round, for it found Valentin high-tailing it round the ring in full flight with Lynch in hot pursuit. Try though he might, Benny just could not land the finisher. Still, he had won handsomely with something to spare, and once again had risen to the occasion.

Now the scorching spotlight of publicity was turned on him with a vengeance. Benny Lynch's epic victory was the main topic of conversation in the factories, workshops and on the street corners. Everyone wanted to know him, or at very least to shake him by the hand. He was their Mr. Big.

CHAPTER EIGHTEEN

GETTING THE FEEL OF FOLDING-MONEY

IT was, I think, fitting that the man who had given Benny his first chance in the big-time should be the one to promote most of the fights which brought him into world prominence. And good old George Dingley was now scouring the globe for opponents who would bring out the best in his money-spinner, and at the same time help to strengthen his claim for a crack at the world title.

Though he was not yet commanding the fabulous purses which were later to be his, Benny was fighting regularly and his financial status was what might be described as comfortable. He had got the feel of folding money, and it was at about this time that he became a car owner; a shiny black showroom piece which, when it made its appearance among the tenements, brought forth the vocal assumption that "it must be the doctor's."

But soon all the kids on the South-side got to know about 'Benny's caur,' and when they came across it parked in some street would at once decide that it needed 'watchun.' The watching process called for strategic positioning and the roof, bonnet and wings were usually well covered when the owner made his appearance to pay-up in the appropriate manner; by throwing his loose change in the air and watching with a wide grin as the urchins scrambled for their fee.

A favourite parking place was Orchard Street, where lived Benny's grandmother, Mrs. Donnelly, on whom the sun rose and set for her devoted grandson. She invariably cautioned him before his bouts to: "Watch your dial, son."

And Benny would dutifully return after each battle, stick his head round the doorway, finger his chin and say: "Look, granny. I've still got ma guid looks!"

The Donnelly home was Lynch's regular port of call every Sunday evening, when the whole family got together in a session of ha'penny rummy. Yet not even Granny Donnelly could prevail on her canny lad to stay later than nine-forty-five, for he was taking his training dead seriously and insisted on being in bed by ten o'clock. Not that the Donnellys' would have wished him to do otherwise, for his welfare was their sole consideration, and indeed their home was to prove a haven of rest for Benny in the dark days which were to come later on.

Following his triumph over Angelmann, the Scot was lined up with Liverpudlian Billy Johnson at the Adelphi Stadium in Glasgow. The latter was no match for hard-hitting Lynch, and the referee wisely stopped the contest in favour of the Glaswegian in the fifth round.

Next Dingley unearthed a real test-piece in Pedrito Ruiz, the flyweight champion of Spain. This would be no 'pushover,' that much was certain, for that doyen of

171

sportsmen, Nick Cavalli, a British agent for continental boxers, intimated that he was willing to wager
that Lynch would finish loser. And Nick's opinion
carried authority, for hadn't he already brought across
Cavagnoli, Huguenin and Angelmann to face the
Gorbals bomber?

The Spaniard was a colourful personality who
attracted much attention as he paraded through the
streets of Glasgow armed with a walking-cane. This
cane, an ornate affair with a curiously shaped head
fashioned in the semblance of a horse, was said to be
his mascot and his constant companion. Pedrito even
took it to the ring with him—not to use, of course, but
just so that he could see it. He was superstitious that
way.

Although plenty of ballyhoo had preceded Ruiz,
Benny first set eyes on his opponent at the weigh-in. He
was short in stature, several inches smaller than Lynch,
but he was equipped with a powerful pair of shoulders
which suggested tremendous punching-power. Benny
watched him fascinated; but it was not the broad shoulders which captured his attention. No, it was the
walking-stick.

Before the fight that evening, Benny called in at his
rival's dressing-room, accompanied by bosom pal Stan
'Sands' Robertson. Ostensibly they had dropped in to
wish Ruiz good hunting, but as they left again, there
was a suspicious bulge beneath Robertson's greatcoat.

Then the balloon went up because Pedrito's cane
had vanished. They searched everywhere, and the
dressing-room was ransacked, but the oh so beautiful
stick was nowhere to be found. The Spanish fighter

was distraught, and made it clear that without his mascot he could not and would not do battle.

On hearing this the promoter who, shrewd bird that he was, already had his suspicions, realised that the matter had gone beyond a joke and made his way to Lynch's quarters. At first Benny, who was enjoying the joke immensely, denied all knowledge of the incident, but when he was informed that Ruiz would not fight unless his beloved cane was retrieved, he reluctantly told his friend to hand it over.

The Scotsman was still chuckling as he made his way to the ring, but the bell soon put a stop to all that. Though he had learned how to mill on the retreat for Valentin Angelmann, Lynch found Ruiz a different proposition altogether for, small as he was, the Spaniard made things even more difficult by moving forwards fast out of a crouch. So that Benny found himself wasting a lot of straight blows on the smoky air of the City Hall or, worse still, connecting off-target with the dangerously hard top of Pedrito's cranium.

He next attempted to solve his problem by upper-cutting but, though he connected frequently, these blows still did not stem the rushes of the rugged little foreigner. It was even-steven at the end of the fourth, for, despite the fact that the pace had never for a moment slackened, Lynch had kept his end up by brilliant defensive boxing, coupled with intermittent rallies at close quarters.

The fifth session saw a change in the fortunes of the fight. At the call of 'time' Ruiz was out of his corner like a flash and charging across the ring like a berserk bull. But instead of taking evasive action, Benny

173

elected to stand his ground and mix it with his muscular adversary. And what a mill followed! For practically the entire three minutes they stood and slugged it out.

First one then the other gained the ascendancy. At one point Lynch was groggy and looked like going down, but he amazingly came back to stagger Pedrito with an all-out assault which he cleverly varied between head and body. The roar of the crowd drowned the sound of the bell, and the referee had to tear them apart and send them to their corners. It was noticeable that wee Benny appeared the fresher of the two.

This was a revelation to his followers, who had hitherto looked on him only as a classy boxer with a useful dig in either hand. Yet here he was introducing himself as a two-handed fighter capable of mixing it with the best of them.

In the sixth Lynch became the aggressor. In fact, from here on it was a one-horse race, for the Spaniard had burned himself out in making his supreme bid for mastery. The Scot went on to win every remaining round, but Ruiz defied all his efforts to land a finisher. The visitor was crafty, and he managed either to slip, duck, guard or ride the more powerful of Benny's shots, though the final bell must have been a welcome sound to him. Thus did a future world champion remove another obstacle from his path to the top.

Less than a week later Benny was again on the job. This time he had to travel south to St. James' Hall, Newcastle, where Peter Miller of Gateshead provided the opposition. A sprightly little fellow and a clever boxer, Miller had stayed almost eight rounds with Lynch on a previous occasion and again he gave the Tyneside crowd moments of exultation in this clash, for he took the first two stanzas clearly. Employing hit-and-run tactics, Peter was in with a blow and away again before Benny could counter.

Warming to his work in the third, Lynch sailed in regardless, throwing vicious hooks with either hand which had Miller in trouble. Peter was again badly belaboured in the fourth, but he was game and he was fit and, though clearly fighting a losing battle, his stamina kept him going.

The seventh saw the beginning of the end, with Miller taking two counts of 'eight' and the next round was the last. The Scot, with a volley of blows, again had his man on the boards, this time out to the wide. But on the towel being skied from the Geordie's corner (today this practice is outlawed) Lynch was named the winner by a technical knockout.

In his next engagement, at the National Sporting Club in Leith, Benny demonstrated his ability to make the most of any opportunity presented him by knocking out Johnny Griffiths of Pontypridd with the first punch of the fight. Someone must have told Johnny that the Glaswegian was a straight-left man, for the Welshman left his corner with his gloves shielding his face to the utter neglect of the downstairs department.

Benny danced around for a moment, possibly thinking this looked too good to be true and suspecting a trap, but still Griffiths kept his hands held high. Wham, came a Lynch special! That vaunted left hook to the stomach and Johnny lost all further interest in the proceedings.

'Southpaws' Benny did not, repeat NOT, like. You

dinna ken why? Well, I'll tell you. Such a fellow is an unorthodox boxer who shapes up with his right fist and foot foremost, and they prove awkward chiefly because the orthodox exponent is not used to dealing with them. Tut Whalley of Hanley came into this category, and he gave the Scot a heap of trouble when they met at the Caird Hall in Dundee.

Whalley was a ringwise customer, and in the early rounds his left swings, coming as they did from an unusual angle, set Lynch back on his heels once or twice. But the Scottish titleholder, realising that he must on no account allow the midlander to get set, set a cracking pace with the object of keeping Tut fully occupied in defending himself.

Not to be outdone, Whalley fought back tooth and nail, and his clever bobbing and weaving made Benny miss badly at times and appear wild. The affray came to a sudden and unsatisfactory end, however, when in the eighth round Whalley swung low and Lynch immediately collapsed in a heap, writhing in agony. Alex Murray, officiating, was left with no option other than to disqualify Whalley.

Though he had a potential world-beater among his flock, Sammy Wilson was not neglecting the rest of the stable. Actually they were better off now than ever before for, with Lynch as the lever, Sammy found promoters more than willing to put his other boys on their bills providing they obtained the services of the bold Benny.

So it came to pass that the Polytechnic was well represented on the Sporting Club's offering in Leith twelve days before Christmas 1934 when Paul Jones,

Bert Nicol, Joe Beckett and Benny Lynch made up one side of the programme. The last-named, however, was the only one to bring home the bacon, which he did by defeating Anglo-Scot Sandy McEwan.

McEwan had been around, and his record included a victory over Young Perez at the time when the latter held the world title, together with a triumph against then current European kingpin, Praxille Gyde. Contrary to expectations, Lynch was not unduly extended and ran out a comfortable points winner at the end of the twelve rounds.

Afterwards it was made known that Benny had damaged his right hand and left forearm in the early rounds. These injuries were the cause of much concern in the Lynch camp, for at this point in his career such setbacks could have had far-reaching consequences. Sammy Wilson was immensely relieved when, after a stringent examination, the specialist pronounced them as being only of a minor nature.

"And will he be able to play the violin?" queried Sammy.

"Yes, of course," replied the medical man.

"That's funny, then," cracked Wilson, "for he couldn't play it before!"

CHAPTER NINETEEN

SO BENNY DID AS HE WAS TOLD

WHAT a momentous year in the life of the kid from the Gorbals was 1935, for it was to bring the fulfilment of even his wildest dreams. Fame, wealth and popularity were all to be his in plenty, yet this year which was to yield so much began by bringing Benny his first severely unfavourable press mention, for on the morning of January 8th the headlines of one national newspaper read: 'Lynch gets verdict — but receives lesson in art of self-defence." Which was not so good for a young man in line for a tilt at the world title.

And who was the guy who had upset the apple-cart? Another contender? Or maybe some continental big-shot? Afraid not. Just another Glasgow boy. Name of Magee. Bobby Magee.

Dapper and debonair, Bobby had met and beaten most of the leading fly and bantamweights in Scotland, but finding it got him nowhere had decided to try his luck south of the border. Making his home in North Shields, he had built up quite a reputation there, fighting in the best company.

Just about the coolest customer competing in any small-hall ring at that time, Magee still had many admirers in Glasgow who believed that he had the beating of Lynch, with the result that the City Hall was packed to the rafters when the pair ducked through the ropes.

Earlier that evening it had seemed doubtful if the fight would go on at all, for while the first preliminary was in progress Magee, who had mislaid his admission ticket, spent some time trying to convince an unsympathetic doorman that he was the fellow scheduled to oppose Lynch.

No good. That doorman had been around. He knew all the tricks of the trade, and this was just about the oldest of the lot.

"I tell you I'm Bobby Magee," the fighter protested vigorously.

"Sure, sure," replied the stalwart sentry on duty. "And I'm Napoleon. Now g'wan beat it!" It looked like a case of no admission and no fight.

Fortunately, some of the late arrivals among the cash customers had recognised Bobby and noticed his plight. They informed promoter Dingley who, already worried stiff at Magee's non-arrival, hastened to the entrance to compliment his aid for conscientiousness and at the same time to bawl him out for lack of observation. Which was something of an injustice, for Magee always dressed immaculately and looked more like a film-star than a professional boxer.

Benny opened fast, cutting out the work and doing nearly all the forcing. But somehow or other his punches didn't land, and those which Bobby couldn't slip or duck he calmly picked off with his gloves.

"Not so guid," Lynch's fans grumbled as he went in again; but again he was made to miss, for those waving arms of Magee had a most annoying habit of being in the right place at the right time. Annoying, that is, from Benny's point of view. He wasn't doing at all well, and as the round came to its close Magee was slipping his left leads with consummate ease before countering with fast, stinging left jabs to the body.

Round two brought no relief to Lynch, for still he was unable to land an authoritative punch. More galling still, at times he was made to miss by the proverbial mile and flounder about like a novice. Magee was boxing calmly and confidently, and his swaying body and fast-moving arms had Benny puzzled and worried. To add to Benny's worries, Bobby was now following some measuring lefts with snappy right crosses.

Things improved somewhat in the third, when Lynch forced his rival backwards round the ring while he slung vicious hooks at him with either hand. It was a short-lived success, though, for Magee cleverly sidestepped to counter with a one-two effort which reined Benny up abruptly. Frustrated, the latter mistakenly sought a breather in a clinch. Only to find that this was like trying to keep out an octopus. Magee was all arms and elbows, and Lynch was completely tied up. His ire rose because Bobby's spoiling was being effected with unruffled calm.

There was a scowl on Benny's face as he went to his corner at the end of the third, and his lips were curled back in anger. Chief second Wilson spotted the danger signals and hastened to caution his charge: "Don't lose your head, son; that's just what he wants. Box him and wait your chance. It'll come." Frustrated, Benny was too het up to listen.

As the bell called the boxers to action for the

180

fourth session, Lynch came out grimly determined to force a way through his rival's tantalising guard and then batter him into the canvas. But the shutters were down at Magee's. Cool as a cucumber, Bobby made play with his evasive tactics and Lynch was quite unable to nail his elusive target. It was too much for Benny.

"Whassa matter with ye, Magee?" he growled. "Why dinna ye stan' up an' fight?"

But the cagey Magee had his man just where he wanted him and, what's more, he knew it.

"Not at all," Bobby quipped. "You're supposed to be the star, so it's up to you to show 'em how good you are."

Benny hurled himself at his taunter, but at close quarters he was about as effective as a one-armed paper-hanger, and must have felt as though he was putting his hands in the blades of a propellor. Was there no escape from or way past Magee's whirling arms?

Our hero was hopping mad when he returned to his corner and, after Sammy Wilson had removed his gumshield, he hissed: "When I do get the measure of this lad I'm really ginny pay him."

Sammy was adamant. "Ye're daft. D'ye no' realise ye're playing right into his barrow? For guidness sake cool off and go out there to box the ears off him." At these words Benny did cool off a little, and the fifth passed without incident. True, Lynch didn't do much, but he didn't give away much either.

This waiting game paid dividends in the sixth, and some of the calm assurance left Magee's features when Lynch got home with a solid left and right to the face. Quick to exploit the advantage, Benny followed up immediately and tagged his man with a combination series before the latter could recover.

Working to orders, Lynch made it long-range stuff at the start of the seventh until, finding the exchanges too slow for his liking, he was tempted and sailed in to have a go, result being that he was again tied up in the all-embracing arms of Magee.

Again Benny began the eighth in more restrained mood, but suddenly a right hook spun him completely round, rocked him badly, but none the less made his blood boil. He came back into the fray like a snarling terrier—though this time with more success, for a left hook to the chin had Magee hanging on desperately at the bell.

The ninth opened with Magee still somewhat befuddled, and Lynch rushed his man to the ropes where he pummelled away full tilt with both hands. Magee, however, was a master at using the ropes for defensive purposes, and there he stood swaying his body, bobbing his head and taking most of the rain of leather on his gloves and forearms.

Both boxers took something of a breather in the tenth, but the proceedings came back to life in the penultimate session which was fought for the most part with Magee's back on the ropes and with Lynch throwing non-stop punches that seldom reached their target. It was the noble art of self-defence at its best. Bobby went right through the card of defensive boxing to the delight of the appreciative audience, and all the while Lynch kept slogging away.

Making his way to his stool at the end of the stanza, Benny must surely have known that the roar of applause which went up was not for him. And that must have been much harder for him to stomach than any punishment Magee could dish out.

Benny toed the line for the twelfth and last minus his gum-shied. This one was for keeps. Straightaway he went after his man, with the sole object of annihilating this will o' the wisp. With flailing fists he went at it in an effort to land just one in the right place; one that would pay for all. But Bobby was still lively and alert, and though Lynch was landing now and then, his best blows were wide of their mark. Then it was all over.

Referee Smith, a Mancunian, totted up his scorecard after which he walked across to Lynch's corner and raised his arm in victory. So everything was all right. Or was it? Opinion was about equally divided as to the merits of this decision; the real point being that even Benny's most ardent supporters had had their confidence in his supposed invincibility more than a trifle shaken. For he certainly hadn't shaped like a potential world champion.

Yet, for his next outing, George Dingley coaxed to Glasgow no less a personage than the world champion himself, Jackie Brown of Manchester, who agreed to trade punches with Benny in a twelve-rounder at eight stone four—four pounds above the championship limit to protect his title.

In view of Benny's showing in the bout with Magee, there was considerable difference of opinion as to the wisdom of this pairing. As it turned out, Lynch supporters needn't have worried.

Their man was at his brilliant best on the night

183

of March 4th at Kelvin Hall. Both men began cautiously, but in the second half of the first round there was a sensation. Springing in, Lynch caught the world champion with a strong right to the jaw and Brown hit the deck. Though he rose immediately, Jackie was clearly dazed and, seizing his opportunity in typical fashion, the Scot got home three more good head punches in jig-time.

Jackie gave him no chance to admire his handiwork, coming back fast to the attack and displaying a bewildering turn of speed and variety of punches. The world champion took the initiative in the next round, and went inside two-fisted to punish Lynch about the body. Benny was glad to resort to long-range exchanges.

Right on top now, Brown measured his man with a left then crossed a lightning right to the jaw. Benny, taken aback, started swinging, but found the Mancunian's defence too tightknit to penetrate, and the latter was scoring freely at the bell.

A series of light lefts to the face were Lynch's contribution in the early moments of the third, but when he switched to the left hook Brown saw it coming and, stepping inside it, rammed home a hard right to the body, then, shifting upstairs, a similar blow to the chin. Again Lynch tried a left hook, but Jackie picked it off in mid-air and countered with a short left to the midsection. Brown, at this time, seemed master of the situation.

Lynch brought the crowd to their feet in the fourth when he connected with a long right hook and again Brown went down. Though Jackie was up before the count could be started, he probably regretted it, for

184

Lynch tore in like a demon, tossing well-directed lefts and rights which did the world ruler no good at all.

Round five saw a thrilling set-to in the centre of the ring in which Lynch came off best. Brown was flying distress signals now, and Benny chased him from pillar to post. Though his defensive work was first-class, Jackie had to take too many strength-sapping body blows for his comfort.

The sixth was Lynch's round too. A worried look-ing Brown, world titleholder or no, had retired into his shell and was boxing almost entirely on the defensive.

Surprisingly enough, he came out of his cover in the next to manoeuvre Lynch on to the ropes and drive home a good solar plexus blow. But it was noticeable that, when the two exchanged punches, it was usually Brown who was the first to break off.

Scottish hopes were sky-high in the eighth when two lefts and a right cross from Lynch had Brown's legs buckling under him. It looked like 'curtains' for Jackie as Benny tore in with flailing arms. But the Mancunian was not king of the world's little men for nothing, and some clever ringcraft got him out of a tight spot.

What a surprise awaited Lynch when he crowded on full sail in the ninth! A fast left-right-left sent the Scot back on his heels, and then we saw some of the stuff that had won the big title for Brown. Before Benny had time to recover, he was being pushed all over the ring on the end of a beautiful straight left. Bump-bump; bump-bump. Brown was thudding home crisp double leads, and the Glaswegian could do nothing about it. No matter how he jerked his head away, that piston-like left continued to find its target. This was undoubtedly Brown's best round, and in it he completely turned the tables.

No time was wasted on science in the tenth. Brown had decided that if Lynch wanted a fight he could have it, and they battled away hammer-and-tongs. There was nothing in it until near the end of the stanza, when Benny had Jackie groping around drunkenly as a result of a left hook.

Brown concentrated on the body in the eleventh, and Benny was subjected to a hammering in this region while he was trapped on the ropes. Working clear, a crashing hook that had all the Scot's weight behind it landed flush on Jackie's jaw. Dazed, the world champion finished the round straddled on the ropes, hands by his sides and practically defenceless. In fact, it seems likely that if the bell had not come when it did, the referee might have been forced to rescue him by stopping the fight and naming Lynch as the winner.

I can disclose for the first time what actually went on in the Scot's corner after that round. I'm sure it will surprise not only lay people but also those who were closely connected with the fight game at the time. Benny sensed that he had Brown at his mercy, and that he could put paid to him in the final session, but Sammy Wilson was almost frantic in his entreaties to Lynch to: "Lay off, ye're miles in front on points anyway."

Sammy finally convinced the fighter in his somewhat crude, but nevertheless effective manner that: "If ye don't bloody well lay-off o' him, son, we'll never get a return for the title!"

So Benny held something back in that final round and, though the crowd roared themselves hoarse as both boys swung heavy punches, little did they realise that only Brown was attempting to hit his full weight.

Though dead tired, Jackie was not yet completely sold out for, as Lynch moved in, the Mancunian met him half-way and swapped punches. Only this time there was no sting behind Brown's blows. Benny had him and he knew it. One solid well-directed punch would do the trick but, for once, he realised that discretion was the better part of valour.

The bell clanged; a breathless hush as they embraced, and then the referee called them both to the centre of the ring and raised the arm of each man aloft in a signal of a drawn decision.

Wilson was staggered, for he felt his man had well won. Benny was near tears, but at least he had something—he had boxed a draw with the champion of the world.

CHAPTER TWENTY

A NEW SENSE OF VALUES

SCOTLAND was now behind Benny to a man. The critics who had lashed him unmercifully for his mediocre showing against Bobby Magee now sang his praises, and the national dailies were chanting these in unison. His fame, which had hitherto been in the main territorial, now extended far beyond the boundaries of his native land. He was on the threshold of universal renown.

Official recognition was quickly forthcoming, and Lynch was nominated to meet Tommy Pardoe of Birmingham, formerly amateur champion five years in succession, in a final eliminator for the right to oppose Brown for the latter's World, British and European titles.

Things were popping fast; perhaps a little too fast for a bewildered young man who was trying hard to adjust his private life to fit in with the demands made on a figure of public importance.

For the record, Benny had at this time just achieved another great ambition with his marriage to — yes, you've guessed it — the girl who was different. For a long time he had found his betrothed very indifferent to his charms, but now Mr. and Mrs. Lynch were busily engaged in setting up house.

Their new home was a modest flat in one of the tenement buildings of Rutherglen Road, mid-way between Sammy Wilson in Florence Street and Granny Donnelly's in Orchard Street. Benny, however, was not permitted too much time to enjoy the pleasures of home life, for his services were much in demand at various functions and, as these were usually all-male affairs, charming Mrs. Lynch frequently found herself sitting by the fireside alone—much more often than either she or Benny would have wished.

Then there was the training. Mr. Lynch could not afford to take any chances for this most important fight, and six o'clock every morning found the Scottish kingpin out doing roadwork, wet or fine, while the afternoons were spent in gymnasium sessions at the Polytechnic.

Rather surprisingly, the Birmingham promoter outbid his Scottish competitors in the matter of a purse offer, which meant that Benny had to travel to the Midland city to do battle at the Embassy Rink on April 15th, less than two weeks after celebrating his twenty-second birthday.

As a result of his assiduous preparation Lynch was in the pink of condition when he and Sammy reached the fight scene. At the weigh-in, Pardoe looked much the frailer of the pair, and it came as a mild surprise when Benny scaled two ounces less than his opponent who tipped the beam at dead on eight stone.

The clash with Pardoe marked another milestone in the journey of our sturdy Scot, for it was his introduction to the big money. Not, perhaps, big money as fighters know it today in an age of inflated prices when managers talk in telephone numbers, but big money for the 1930's. As eventual victor, Lynch received £360, his biggest purse to date.

Of course, this was chicken-feed compared to the purses which he was to collect later, but it gave him an entirely new sense of values, one which he could very well have done without. He was nothing if not generous, and soon it became known that Benny was a good 'tap' — which means that seldom did anyone approach him with a hard luck story and leave empty-handed.

Another incident concerning this fight is worthy of note, because for the first time for years Lynch was floored. The indignity occurred in the dying seconds of the first round, when Pardoe connected with a right to the chin, and Benny went crashing to the boards. As he fell, the Scot's head hit the ring floor with a resounding thump, but just then the bell sounded the end of the session and Benny rose smartly enough, apparently recovered though he at first made for his opponent's corner rather than his own.

Seems that bump on the head started something which Benny was to pay for dearly later on with recurring violent headaches and periodic dizzy spells. Could the incident have had any bearing on the fighter's future behaviour?

Certainly he became a man of moods; at one moment his normal cheery self, at another a morbid groucher. It was much later that those closest to him learned that Lynch spent many a night pacing the floor, wringing his hands in anguish, willing to do anything that would ease the pains in his head—anything, that is, except see a doctor. Such a person would probably have ordered him to hospital, and with the world title almost within his grasp Benny just couldn't take time off. So the headaches were thrust to one side, and the few who knew of their existence were sworn to secrecy.

However, to get back to the bout itself. The more sturdily-built Lynch was faster and displayed the better repertoire of punches in the opener, until that Pardoe right out of the blue sent him sprawling.

Tommy found himself pinned on the ropes early in the second, but Benny was too eager to land a haymaking hook and left himself open for the Birmingham man to counter with a short right uppercut to the heart. Lynch was playing the role of the hunter, with the taller Pardoe, possessing as he did the longer reach, picking his punches well and always preferring to keep the exchanges at long range.

Pardoe was content to remain on the defensive in the third and, although Lynch connected with a number of good body blows, the Brum boy's left leads were crisp and accurate and sent the visitor's head back repeatedly. Lynch was rather erratic, and again took a right cross to the jaw which visibly shook him.

Predominant factor in the fourth was some clever feinting and drawing by the midlander. Benny was continually foxed into leading and often had to take sizzling cross counters for his folly. In the last minute of the session he became wild, leaving his guard wide open and allowing Pardoe to jump in and out quickly with more lefts to the face. Finding his long range efforts unsuccessful, Benny tried conclusions at close quarters, but again drew a blank. The Englishman had all the answers.

Lynch rallied well in the fifth and, bringing his left hook into action, scored hurtfully to the stomach. Tommy tried retreating, but was on the receiving end of more hooks until he opened up with his usual last-minute rally. This time, though, Pardoe was made to miss badly by some clever Lynch headwork, and now the latter was definitely coming into the picture.

Close-quarter work was the feature of the sixth, Lynch's strength and heavier punching taking the honours and forcing Pardoe to give ground. But when he did so heavy hooking downstairs clearly had him worried.

The Birmingham man made Lynch come to him in the seventh. The policy paid dividends towards the end of the stanza when Benny, frustrated at having to do all the leading, slung an overhand right. With perfect technique, Tommy blocked the blow and then stepped in to rip home three stinging lefts.

Round eight was the Scot's best to date. Full of confidence, he slung a left uppercut which rocked Pardoe to his heels, followed with a scything right and finished with a left hook to the jaw which dropped his rival. But the ex-amateur could take it. He rose at 'three' and, though dazed, stalled his way out of further trouble until the end of the round.

Sensing victory, Lynch tore into his man in the ninth and that lethal left hook to the guts brought an audible gasp from the Brummie and a prolonged o-o-ooh from the crowd. Such blows were taking their toll, and as the round drew to its close a left and right again sent Pardoe down on his backside. Yet though he had taken plenty, Tommy was still full of fight and was up without waiting for a count.

Following up the good work in the ensuing round, Lynch punished his adversary freely both to head and body. Pardoe's features were a bloody mask now, left eye cut badly, nose and mouth both bleeding freely. Weak though he was, though, Tommy continued to box cleverly and to give his all. He earned a round of applause when he made the eager Scot miss by feet with some clever footwork.

Benny was looking almost as fresh as when he started at the end of the eleventh and, though he had had to take some Pardoe counters in his efforts to connect with his own pile-drivers, there was now little force behind Tommy's shots and Lynch was able to shrug them off.

Making an amazing recovery in the twelfth, Pardoe conserved his remaining energy well and, though periodically badly shaken, he suddenly produced a perfect right cross which landed flush on the point of Lynch's chin.

That very fact must have been heartbreaking to Tommy, for it did not even check Benny's forward advance. Now, however, the former did not retreat, but raised English hopes by standing like a tiger at bay, trading punches with his tormentor. Despite his brave front, it was clear to those at the ringside that Tommy had shot his bolt.

What purgatory the thirteenth session must have been to the bemused and battered midlander. He was chased and subjected to a terrific shellacking throughout, only his fighting heart keeping him going.

Scotland's pride was not to be denied, and he finally felled Pardoe and put him half-way through the ropes with a smashing left hook. Incredibly, courageous Tommy staggered to his feet at 'two,' and somehow survived the remainder of the round.

But the pay-off was not long delayed. Lynch, a punching machine, battered his foe savagely again in the fourteenth, thudding in blows to the midriff which left Tommy looking like a reed swaying in the wind.

How Pardoe remained upright was a miracle, but the red badge of courage was on him for all to see in the form of his own blood. He was through and he was finished. Everyone in the place knew it except Tommy Pardoe, for he was squinting through glazed eyes trying to find the outline of his adversary who was chastising him so unmercifully. No, it was not Tommy's night.

As the Scot came boring in, Pardoe fell back on the ropes where Lynch continued his work of destruction. And that's how it finished, for though Tommy didn't know the meaning of the word 'surrender' his seconds did, and they performed their work of mercy in the nick of time.

The end of the long Lynch trail to the top was at last in sight. Benny had done it again. The last hurdle had been cleared. A title tilt at Brown, involving each of the northerner's three championships, had become a reality.

Though Benny was a huge draw anywhere in Scotland, Brown was equally so in his native Manchester and, as he was the champion who would be accommodating a challenger, the meeting was almost certain to take place south of the border. Loyal Sammy Wilson felt he owed it to his brother Scots to parade his pride and joy before them once more before Lynch settled down to condition himself for the great event.

And so it came about that, three weeks after the Pardoe affray, Benny was pitted against a Welsh ringster named Billy Hazel in a scheduled ten-rounder, and the partisan Glasgow fans flocked to pass judgment on their candidate for world honours.

They had little opportunity for criticism, for Benny punched his opponent into insensibility in the very first round. The opposition provided was not strong enough —although it is doubtful if anyone in the world at the weight could have stood up to Lynch at this period, for the Scot was now at his finest both as a boxer and as a puncher.

Bring on the champion! Even now some of the critics were not too enthusiastic about Benny's chances of lifting the laurels. Sure, he had already drawn with Brown, but that had been an overweight affair and Jackie may not have been too fit. This time, they opined, he'd be right on his toes.

They didn't know the true facts about the previous meeting of which I wrote earlier, and Brown was made an odds-on favourite in the pre-fight wagering as soon as the match was clinched for Belle Vue, Manchester, on September 9th, 1935.

And that is where we came in.

AFTERWORD

SCOTLAND has bred some of the finest eight-stone men ever to grace a boxing ring – to name but a few Tancy Lee (1915), Elky Clark (1924), Johnny Hill (1927), Benny Lynch, Jackie Paterson (1939) and Walter McGowan (1963). Champions all, yet by far the greatest was Lynch. Invincible against any flyweight the world could pit against him in his heyday, Benny was yet defenceless against his inner-self.

Over the years many boxing champions have ridden the dizzy heights blissfully unaware that they cannot abuse nature for ever. Eventually the pay-off has struck like a thief at night and, next morning, their world has lain in pieces leaving them to totter along the already over-crowded rings of Mugs' Alley.

There have been many tragedies of, and in, the roped arenas but the sudden decline and fall of Benny Lynch, once the pride of Scotland, surpasses any other such drama because the wee man turned his back on fame, fortune, a world crown, good health and self-respect when at the peak of his career. Even today he could still have been among us for did not Jimmy Wilde, the diminutive Welshman with whom Benny will always be compared, continue into his late seventies?

The lad from the Gorbals should have become a memorial to the supreme sporting stock produced by Britain and, in the latter half of his life, he could have

197

matured into being a wealthy and respected citizen. Instead poor Lynch, once a pocket-Hercules, lost everything including his very life. A coincidental irony of fate is that Benny and Anne's eldest son, John, died in his early thirties like his father and was buried in the same grave at Christmas 1970.

My hope is that, within the pages of this book, I did not dwell too long on the human weaknesses and the ultimate failure of such a wonderful Scotsman. I wanted people to know about his basic greatness, his fairness inside the ropes, his ability to box like a wizard and hit with the power of a sledgehammer. Perhaps, above all, it should be borne in mind that wee Benny never had the chance to defend himself against the many allegations written about him. Also, that he never deliberately harmed anyone apart from himself.

Had he been born in a different environment or been blest with stronger will-power through which to protect himself from the evil influence of some acquaintances, the foregoing story would surely have been very different. And, had he been boxing today, he would have been the televised idol of the world's millions.

Yet I believe that Benny rests content in the hope that his meteoric rise to fame may serve as an example to aspiring youngsters . . . and that his end may serve as a warning to all those who tread the glory road.